P9-CEV-180

Why
GUYS
Need God

Mike Erre

HARVEST HOUSE PUBLISHERS

EUGENE, OREGON

All Scripture quotations are taken from the Holy Bible: NEW INTERNATIONAL VERSION®. NIV®. Copyright © 1973, 1978, 1984 by the International Bible Society. Used by permission of Zondervan. All rights reserved.

Published in association with the Conversant Media Group, P.O. Box 3006, Redmond, WA 98007.

Michael Erre: Published in association with the literary agency of Mark Sweeney & Associates, 28540 Altessa Way, Ste. 201, Bonita Springs, FL 34135

ConversantLife.com is a trademark of Conversant Media Group. Harvest House Publishers, Inc., is a licensee of the trademark ConversantLife.com.

Cover by Abris, Veneta, Oregon

WHY GUYS NEED GOD
Copyright © 2008 by Mike Erre
Published by Harvest House Publishers
Eugene, Oregon 97402
www.harvesthousepublishers.com

Library of Congress Cataloging-in-Publication Data
Erre, Mike, 1971-
Why guys need God / Mike Erre.
    p. cm.
Includes bibliographical references.
ISBN-13: 978-0-7369-2126-8
ISBN-10: 0-7369-2126-5
    1. Men (Christian theology) 2. Masculinity—Religious aspects—Christianity. 3. Christian men—Religious life. I. Title.
    BT703.5.E77 2008
    248.8'42—dc22
                                                    20070303200

All rights reserved. No part of this publication may be reproduced, stored in a retrieval system, or transmitted in any form or by any means—electronic, mechanical, digital, photocopy, recording, or any other—except for brief quotations in printed reviews, without the prior permission of the publisher.

Printed in the United States of America

08 09 10 11 12 13 14 15 16 / VP-SK / 11 10 9 8 7 6 5 4 3 2

Download a Deeper Experience

Mike Erre is part of a faith-based online community called ConversantLife.com. At this website, people engage their faith in entertainment, creative arts, science and technology, global concerns, and other culturally relevant topics. While you're reading this book, or after you have finished reading, go to www.conversantlife.com/mikeerre and use these icons to read and download additional material from Mike that is related to the book.

 Resources: Download study guide materials for personal devotions or a small-group Bible study.

 Videos: Click on this icon for interviews with Mike and video clips on various topics.

 Blogs: Read through Mike's blog and articles and comment on them.

 Podcasts: Stream ConversantLife.com podcasts and audio clips from Mike.

conversant **life** .com

engage your faith

To Nathan and Hannah

I hope you know how much your
daddy longs to live up to these words.

and

to Carl T. Erre (1940–2007)

I miss you, Pop.

Acknowledgments

Many thanks to...

Casey, Mike, Huy, Mark, Greg, and Brent	for shaping this book
Stan, Bruce, and Mark	for dreaming big dreams
Ian and Doug	for reading ugly first drafts
Ted	for helping me see how weakness is strength
The 4 Horsemen	for many hours of wasteful (but needed) escape
J.P.	for showing me how real men love Jesus
Krysti	for fantastic editorial help
My family	for always believing in me
Justina	for unwavering love and patience
Gary and Pete	for keeping me on the straight and narrow
The elders, staff, and men of Rock Harbor	for allowing me the grace to grow up on the job
The Joens family	for being family away from family

and to the many scholars, authors, and teachers whose work is represented in this book, for helping me along the road to finding freedom to be a guy who needs God.

Contents

WHY THERE ARE
BOOKS FOR MEN

> The longing to be alive is drowned by lesser ambitions. On most days, we just want to do the routine, make ends meet, dodge the bullets, and make it through. We think we are alive, yet we merely exist. We have traded the authentic for the imitation.
>
> ERWIN RAPHAEL McMANUS

I love all things Star Wars. I have enjoyed watching the old movies hundreds of times. I have waited in line for the new ones. In between, I have read the books and played the video games. I love these movies because they remind me of one of the most indelible images of my childhood. In a scene from the first Star Wars movie (*Episode IV: A New Hope*), Luke Skywalker has just learned from his uncle that he has to stay home and work instead of leaving to join the rebellion. He stands outside his home and longingly stares at the twin suns of Tatoonie as they set. The John Williams score works its magic, and I am hopelessly hooked.

The music, the visuals, and the look on Luke's face all put me in touch with one concept: *yearning.* I was too young to understand it at the time, but that image would define my life as a man. The message of that moment (for Luke and for me) contained two simple truths:

There is more.

I am missing it.

I felt that way as an adolescent in junior high and high school, as a college student, and as I began exploring a career. I feel that way now as a young dad, husband, and pastor. That haunted feeling has never gone away. And in every book I read that is written for and about men from a Christian perspective, I find the same message on every page, this time directed to me as a man:

There is more (to being masculine).

I am still missing it.

This inner inadequacy shows itself everywhere. My friend Pete plays guitar, writes music, tends roses, smokes cigars, builds stuff, and even has a cool accent. He is handsome (chicks dig him), and he is an athlete. I spend time with him and am reminded that I am not really any of those things.

My friend Todd is ultracompetitive, wins at most things he tries, and projects confidence and strength to those around him. Being around him reminds me that I am too emotional and lose at most things I try.

My friend Chad is funny, sensitive, intelligent, and the most creative guy I've ever met. Again, in comparison, I am 0-for-4.

Shawn, another friend, is just cool. Looks cool. Has cool hair. Loves cars. Can do almost anything. Me: no hair, no coolness, and can do just about anything...with the yellow pages.

The plumber reminds me I don't know plumbing. The mechanic reminds me I don't know cars. Outdoorsmen remind me I don't know camping. Brokers remind me I don't know stocks. And the church? The fact that women vastly outnumber men in our churches has been well documented—and doesn't surprise me.[1] Men don't need another place that reminds us of how we don't measure up.

Over and over again, I have these Luke Skywalker moments of yearning: There is more to being a man, and I am missing it. I should know how to change the oil in my car, write plays, hunt elk, catch salmon, and cook steaks. But I don't. I talk for a living. That is what I am good at. If you need a good talker, I'm your guy.

But here's the interesting thing: Pete, Todd, Chad, and Shawn all feel the same way. None of them measure up as men in their own eyes. They all beat themselves up (even Pete!) about how they should be more masculine and better at this or that.

I've gotten to know some men who are incredibly wealthy. They feel this yearning too. And so do professional musicians, athletes, and CEOs. In fact, I think this belief is universal among men: *There is more, and I am missing it. I should be more of a man (in whatever way), but I'm not.*

The vast majority of men's books, conferences, small groups, and retreats all reinforce the same message. They hold out a masculine ideal and inspire us to go after it: four principles of courage. Ten steps to business success. Creative ways to romance our wives. We are to find adventure, fight a battle, or win a beauty. We have promises to keep and sacrifices to make. And to top it all off, we need to be more like Jesus.

I need to protect, provide, spiritually lead my family, do my work with integrity, be generous with my money, coach my kid's soccer team, and romance my wife—all while avoiding porn. I need to go to church regularly, belong to a men's accountability group, read my Bible and pray daily, and help around the house.

Who lives up to this?

If we are honest, we need something new and different to aim our lives toward. Something big enough to capture all of masculinity and vigorous enough to fight the lies we hear in church and from the world.

The whole Luke Skywalker thing is, for me, a picture of the masculine condition. I should be more, but I am not. There is more out there—real life, real manhood, whatever—but I am missing it. And I'm tempted to think that more money, more sex, more acclaim, more status, more toys, more kids, more _____ will help.

But it won't.

I've heard it said that the masculine condition is due to the feminization of the church or Christianity. Or that the gender wars and women's movement have left men confused.

But I don't think so.

I think it is God's fault. I think God set men up to need books about what it means to be a man. God is the author of the masculine condition. Not women, not men, not the church, not the culture, but God Himself.

And understanding that is the first and most important step toward recovering an authentic masculinity and *living* as men rather than merely existing.

Part One

THE JOURNEY

Chapter 1

IN THE IMAGE

I want to examine what "meaning of life" books typically overlook. They are right to tell us we are created for worship, ministry, evangelism, fellowship, and discipleship, but they are wrong to stop there. Look at the list again. While it more or less covers our responsibilities as Christians, it says little about what it means to be human. Does our purpose for life consist entirely in these spiritual activities, or is there also some value in showing up for work, waxing our car, playing with our children, or taking a trip to the beach—just a few of the many things we do, not because we are Christian, but because we are human?

MICHAEL E. WITTMER

Is it me, or does the whole "what does it mean to be a man" conversation seem pretty strange? I don't see a lot of books for women defining true femininity, but the shelves of bookstores are stocked with loads of guidance on how to be a man. Women just seem to know what it is to be a woman. From what I can see, most of their questions have to do with *Will people love and delight in me as the woman I am?* and not about what it means to be a woman in the first place.

Not true with fellas. Men have angst that books and retreats and conferences on masculinity tap into. We don't know what it means to be real men. The numbers of us raised in homes with no father, an absent father, a preoccupied and distant father, or an abusive father are pretty staggering. So that sets us up for failure right from the start.

To Be or Not to Be

Into this vacuum of masculinity step many competing images and ideas. The world around us portrays manly men ranging from tough guys (John Wayne, Clint Eastwood, Bruce Willis) to bad boys (Johnny Depp, Russell Crowe, Mel Gibson) to sweet, sensitive types (Hugh Grant) to class clowns (Ben Stiller, Will Ferrell). And then there are jocks (Michael Jordan, Tom Brady, Cal Ripken), rock stars (Bono, Sting, Bruce Springsteen), and CEOs (Donald Trump, Bill Gates).

Not enough options? Need more choices? With all of those conflicting images, no wonder men have a tough time figuring out what it means to really be a man.

We need to differentiate between maleness and masculinity. Leon Podles offers this helpful insight:

> Maleness and masculinity are not the same thing. We commonly recognize a distinction between facts of biology and masculine identity. Simply being an adult male is not enough; one must in addition be a man, which means more than simply having a male body...Sex is what the body is, that is, male or female. Gender is everything that is not limited to the body...maleness is a physical quality, masculinity a cultural and spiritual one, although one that is connected with the physical realities of being male.[1]

The church throws its own male stereotypes into the ring—beginning with its characterization of Jesus, a nice, Mr. Rogers kind of guy. In our quest to keep Jesus divine, we have minimized the fact that He was a man.

The masculine images from my upbringing in the church ranged from the nice, polite (never offensive or passionate) sermons given by the nice, polite pastor, to the soft and warm handshakes given by the ushers who collected the money. Sex was never mentioned. Anger, ambition, and competition were never discussed. The not-so-subtle message was that Jesus made us into nice men who were sweet to our wives, read the Bible to our kids, and kept out of trouble. The problem was that this isn't what Jesus was like or what He said. (As Philip Yancey pointed out, nobody would crucify Mr. Rogers.)

I remember our youth pastor getting fired because he dared to take his suit off during the sermon (he was wearing a pair of shorts and a T-shirt underneath) to make the point that God isn't particularly impressed with our external appearance. But apparently, the church was, so the guy was let go. I grew up thinking that church (and therefore Jesus and the rest of Christianity) was boring and irrelevant, but it was a great place to make out with girls.

I went to college and learned that men were responsible for a lot of the trouble the world was in. Some of my professors said it was chauvinistic to call God "Father" and to refuse to let women be pastors and speakers. They said men were war-mongering, womanizing, oppressive, and dominating. I felt as if I needed to apologize for being a man.

In my Christian campus groups, men were never called out to really be men. We were asked to "initiate" with women (meaning it was the guys' job to ask the "sisters" out) and to be responsible for DTR (what our little Christian circle called "defining the relationship"). We were told not to masturbate or look at porn, and to watch how far we went with girls. That was pretty much it.

So here was my situation: zero help from the world. Zero help from the church. Zero help from my friends. Zero help from girls. And a hole in my spirit that kept saying, *There is such a thing as true masculinity, and you don't have it.*

I remember sitting up late in my room as a college student listing out all my masculine options: Should I be a jock? Or maybe play up the intellectual side? Should I be rebellious? Or really work on my "walk with Jesus"? And my decisions were almost entirely based on getting girls. Whatever they would want me to be, I would endeavor to be. I literally wrote this out at the time in my journal. I had no idea. I had no one to turn to for understanding or advice. Not knowing who I was (and was supposed to be), I let majority vote determine my actions. But I also knew that as things stood, I wasn't cool enough, spiritual enough, talented enough, or good-looking enough on my own. What I really needed was to act like somebody else.

The point is this: If we go into the world or the church looking for images of what it means to be a man, we will come away confused. We hear one thing from the world, another from the church, and still another from the academy. We have a bewildering array of options. And if family, schools, movies, friendships, and churches won't (and ultimately can't) define masculinity for us, where can we find the answers we still need?

Made in the Image

After college, I stumbled into the opening pages of the Bible and read the story I had often seen reenacted on the Sunday school flannel-graph board but had not yet fully understood:

> Then God said, "Let us make man in our image, in our likeness, and let them rule over the fish of the sea and the birds of the air, over the livestock, over all the earth, and over all the crea-tures that move along the ground." So God created man in his own image, in the image of God he created him; male and female he created them (Genesis 1:26-27).

The poetry and rhythm of Genesis 1 culminate in this declaration of God to create humanity. As part of the material, physical creation, human beings are declared to be "very good." It is a good thing to be creaturely—to be made of physical stuff. Yet for centuries after the coming of Jesus, the early church had to fight against teachings that diminished the role of the physical world and that inappropriately elevated the spiritual world. A theology of creation shows us that being created and being made of physical stuff is a good thing. Not only that, it shows us we can love and enjoy the natural world without making it an object of worship. Certainly the heavens declare God's glory, but they are not God Himself.

The New Testament emphatically teaches that the physical things of this world are good and that we can enjoy them within the bounds of God's law.[2] We need this reminder; even centuries later, the people of God still are tempted to think the spiritual is separate from or in opposition to the physical. For example, many still distinguish spiritual activities from nonspiritual ones, spiritual jobs from nonspiritual ones, and spiritual relationships from nonspiritual ones. As we will see, none of these distinctions exist in the Bible.

Human beings are made in the image of God; men and women are not God, but only images of God. As image bearers, human beings stand at the pinnacle of the created order. But we are still part of creation, made from the dust of the earth, and we cannot rightly claim our own independence and autonomy. For humanity to flourish as God intended, we must keep our exalted status and our humble dependence in tension.

Against those who place little value on human life and dignity, we assert the fundamental truth that all human beings are made in God's image and are worthy of respect and protection. But against those who assign humanity an almost godlike status, we remind ourselves that our freedom is limited and that our personhood is ultimately God's gift to us.

Men were made in God's image. The Hebrew words for *image* (*tselem*) and *likeness* (*demuth*) both refer to the practice of Ancient Near Eastern kings building or carving out images of themselves in order to represent their power and authority over their far-flung empires, even if they were not physically present. These images represented the absolute dominion of the ruler over the areas he controlled.

In the same way, human beings were created to reflect central features about the nature of God. We represent Him to some degree. Men and women are not gods themselves, but they reflect something of His nature.

Notice too that God placed His glory in the image of the man and woman together.[3] Both are needed to fully reflect what God is like. This is often overlooked. The Bible seems to begin with absolute unity and equality while still allowing for difference and distinction.

By examining the opening pages of Genesis, we begin to get an idea of what it means to be masculine. We see expressions of community, sexuality, work and vocation, and spirituality, all within the first two chapters.

But the main point of this chapter is that all other images of masculinity will fail us. None of us will be sufficient to carry the weight of life in this world as a man and as a disciple of Jesus unless we start here first. God begins by saying that masculinity (and femininity, but that is a different book) is part of God's good creation.

Starting in Genesis 1, God teaches us something important: God loves what He has made. He delights, rejoices, and revels in it.[4] To be a part of God's creation is a wonderful thing, and human beings stand at the top of it all. Every other living thing in Genesis 1 is made "according to its [own] kind." Only human beings are made as an expression of God's kind—that is, in His image. The literary structure of Genesis 1 changes at the creation of humanity. Instead of a divine command, "Let there be man and woman," we read about God's creative process and the material He used to create man and woman. These stylistic changes are to show us that human beings have a special place in creation and that they are uniquely able to relate to God and to each other.[5]

Most Christian discussions of gender start in Genesis 3 with the fall of Adam and Eve. This is a tragic mistake. Yes, masculinity has been marred and the image of God tarnished in us by the entrance of sin and death into the world. But we can't start in Genesis 3 if we want to discover what the Bible says about what it means to be a man. If we begin that late in the story, we miss the glimpses of what God had in mind when He created man. We also can't account for the fact that Jesus' work in this world is much greater than simply forgiving sins: Jesus is at work to restore creation to God's original design and intent. The New Testament includes admonitions to men that reflect this plan and that don't make sense apart from it.

So our story begins in Genesis 1–2 with the declaration that it is good to be male. It is good to be a man regardless of what kind of man you are. You may think this is obvious, but our world and our churches often say otherwise. In order to be a man in this world (and in most churches) we are encouraged to tone down our masculine impulses. This isn't a wholly bad thing, but the line between asking us to tone down those impulses or to get rid of them altogether is a fine one. Sometimes men are made to feel that our very nature is wrong and that we are the sole source of the world's problems.

Though the vast majority of church leadership is male, the primary expressions of worship and spirituality are feminine. I don't love my dad or my friends by closing my eyes and raising my hands to the sky while singing, "I'm desperate for you," or "You are the air I breathe." I can do this toward God sometimes, but at other times, I'd like to worship Him a little more actively. I don't naturally gravitate toward having quiet times with Jesus, where I simply bask in His love. My biological dad and I don't bask in each other's love. We go fishing. I'd like to go fishing with Jesus.

More than any recent Christian author, John Eldredge has tapped into this reality. He reminds us of the fierce and wild God of the Scriptures and the untamed revolutionary named Jesus, both of whom encourage men to worship as men.

Yes, we begin with the simple truth that being a man is a good thing. We don't have anything to apologize for. Our desires for sex, success, significance, and competition are good things if we direct them properly. The fact that my boy loves to throw rocks and jump off stuff (all while attempting to do great bodily harm to his dad) is a good thing. Yes, we are sinful and tarnished. But the fall has not pushed out all the goodness of God's creation.[6]

We acknowledge all the hurt and pain that men have caused in the past: the oppression of women and minorities, the chauvinism disguised as Christian theology, and our absence from our homes and families (regardless of whether we were physically there). At the same time, we affirm that masculinity itself is not the issue. Rather, masculinity that is functioning outside of God's intent is behind these things.

We begin by reminding ourselves that our maleness and our masculinity are good things! We begin by expressing gratitude for how God has made and designed us. We begin, not by looking to Hollywood, or Washington DC, or even our own families for an image of what it means to be masculine. We begin by placing ourselves back when the universe was new and unblemished, when God revealed His design for men in the way He created Adam and in what He called Adam to do.

Men and God

What follows from this is that there is such a thing as a masculine spirituality—a way that men distinctively approach and worship God that is different from feminine spirituality.

> Perhaps the term [masculine spirituality] sounds new, strange or even wrong or unnecessary. Why would we bother speaking of a spirituality that is especially masculine or male? Is there anything to be learned here? Don't we all come to God the same way? I am convinced that there are different paths because men and women pay attention to different things. Moviemakers know that, book publishers know that, advertisers know that, salespersons know that, almost everybody knows that except the clergy. Fortunately, it is strongly validated in universal sacred stories, legends and myths, which are invariably written for men or women, and different patterns are found in the Judeo-Christian Scriptures, too.[7]

Distinctively masculine ways of relating to God do exist. This should not surprise us, for the equality we see in Genesis 1–2 does not equate to sameness between the sexes. If God merely wanted companionship for Adam, He Himself could have provided it. If He had wanted fraternity, He would have created another man. Instead, He made a woman—equality with a difference and distinction, psychologically and biologically.

For women and men to be equal does not imply that they must be identical. This, of course, parallels the most fundamental of Christian ideas about God: that God is triune. God is three persons who live simultaneously and equally as one essence. We clearly see equality within the nature of God, yet we also see differences in functions and roles.[8]

As we will explore in more detail, to be a man is to relate to God in certain ways—ways that are no better or worse than the ways women relate to God. Part of our gender confusion, however, has led us to compare masculine and feminine spiritualities and to make judgments between them. The scriptural distinctions between male and female are grounded in these early chapters in Genesis. They were not intended to allow one sex to claim superiority over the other. Both men and women are image bearers, both have intrinsic dignity and worth, and both play unique parts in God's world. Only our modern reactions against role distinctions prevent us from seeing that men and women have different kinds of honor.

G.K. Chesterton wrote a short poem entitled "Comparisons" that describes our problem:

> If I set the sun beside the moon,
> And if I set the land beside the sea,
> And if I set the town beside the country,
> And if I set the man beside the woman,
> I suppose some fool would talk about one being better.[9]

To present a masculine spirituality is not to discount a feminine spirituality. It simply seeks to give men permission to worship and live in the ways God intended. That permission is sorely lacking in the world and the church, but it is urgently needed.

David Murrow presents a compelling case for a masculine spirituality in *Why Men Hate Going to Church*. His comments are worth quoting at length:

> Today's church does not mesmerize men; it repels them. Just 35 percent of the men in the United States say they attend church weekly. In Europe, male participation rates are much worse, in the neighborhood of 5 percent. This hardly sounds like a male-dominated, patriarchical institution to me...Today's church has developed a culture that is driving men away. Almost every man in America has tried church, but two-thirds find it unworthy of a couple of hours once a week.
>
> When men need spiritual sustenance, they go to the wilderness, the workplace, the garage, or the corner bar. They watch their heroes in the stadium or on the racetrack. They plunge into a novel or sneak off to a movie. Church is one of the last places men look for God...
>
> The answer is not a male-dominated church. The answer is a balanced approach: teaching practices, and opportunities that allow for both masculine and feminine expressions in the church...I am not calling men back to the church. Instead, I am calling the church back to men...Few churches model men's values: risk and reward, accomplishment, heroic sacrifice, action and adventure...He finds church dull for the same reason he finds chick flicks dull: neither one reflects his masculine heart...[Men] have no desire to fall in love with a wonderful man, even one named Jesus...
>
> Like most men, he does not possess the natural gifts that make a good churchgoer. He's not very expressive, verbal, or sensitive. He's not a very good teacher or singer. He's uncomfortable praying aloud or holding hands with strangers.[10]

Murrow points to a study that concludes, "While the US population is split fairly evenly between men and women, there are more women (61%) than men (39%) in the pews. The difference is found in every age category."

The point, again, is to find balance and permission for men and women to approach God in the ways most natural to His design. In reacting to the abuses and falsehoods of male-dominated 1950s-style Christianity, we have overcorrected. The best way to honor the dignity and value of women is for men to be real, authentic men.

The blurring of gender distinctions has come at great cost. The generations following us are not more free or at peace because of our revamped definitions of men and women. We see greater confusion, not less. We do not know what it means to be masculine. If increased occurrences of abuse, immorality, divorce, homosexuality, and suicide are reliable indicators, then for all of our political correctness and gender discussion, we are not better off.

Instead of diminishing gender distinctions, the Bible insists on them. Adam and Eve were created differently and were designed to be complementary to each other. In a sense, each was designed to complete (that is, to cover the weaknesses) of the other. In the New Testament, Paul gives different instructions to men and women, husbands and wives. Regardless of how we understand those instructions today, we cannot consistently believe that the Scriptures show no difference between men and women and their roles in society.[11] They are equal, but that doesn't mean they are the same. Differentiated roles were corrupted by humanity's fall into sin, not created by it.

Stu Weber makes this point well: "Gender is primarily an issue of *theology*. And theology is the most foundational of all sciences. Gender is at the heart of creation. Gender is tied to the image of God. Gender is central to the glory of God."[12]

This goes against the prevailing attitudes of our politically correct, nonoffensive, modern sensibilities. But we must follow this path for the good of the many men, both within the church and outside of it, who desperately are looking for some way to understand what it means to be masculine.

For example, women don't go around insulting each other by saying, "You're such a man." They don't encourage each other in hardship with the challenge to be a woman. But men do this kind of thing all the time. Be a man, don't be a baby, don't be a mama's boy, take your skirt off. These insults make a serious point: We may not know what a man is, but we all know what a man isn't. One of the worst insults a guy can receive is to be told that he is playing like a girl.

So we spend most of our lives proving to ourselves that we are men. We make money, chase status symbols, conquer projects and beautiful women, or withdraw from competition altogether. But underlying all these pursuits is the quest to prove ourselves. We can't help it.

The point is simply this: Maleness and femaleness extend beyond the body and into the soul.[13] The differences of our reproductive organs represent differences in how we function in the world and how we relate to each other and to God. Being a man isn't a bad thing. And we should encourage the full range of masculine spiritual expression in the quest to become more like Jesus.

We will look at this masculine spirituality in three areas: in the field (issues of work and business), in the bedroom (issues of sexuality), and in the arena (issues of relationship). In each area, we'll examine the Bible's teachings through the following grid:

- Creation: What can we learn from Genesis 1–2 about what God intended for men?

- The fall: What do the curses and judgments of Genesis 3 tell us about how God's design has been tarnished in men?

- Redemption: How do the teachings of Jesus and Paul help us as Christ followers and men to live in a fallen world in ways that please God?

Chapter 2

ON BEING STRONG AND COURAGEOUS

Until a man learns to deal with the fact that life is hard, he will spend his days chasing the wrong thing, using all his energies trying to make life comfortable, soft, nice, and that is no way for any man to spend his life.

JOHN ELDREDGE

Reality bites. I never saw the movie that went by that title, but I agree with the concept. The older I get, the more I realize that the dreams and ambitions of my youth are nothing but fluff and vapor. I have learned quite painfully that God, the universe, other people, traffic, disease, death, love, risk, pain, and depression all refuse to bend to my will. Regardless of how much I try to negotiate, bargain, manipulate, plead, or rage against them, they won't budge.

And I suppose this simple truth is what fuels a bewildering (and in some cases bizarre) array of options for escape from reality.

If your marriage needs spicing up, we have online porn. If you are into sports, we have fantasy football, baseball, basketball, and even *golf* (I didn't believe it at first). Bored or unhappy? Millions find solace in online gaming communities, adopting custom-designed avatars to present to the world. We have online dating (Hi, I'm Mike, and I'm young and skinny with a full head of hair), online gambling, and count-less other escapes from real life. If reality disappoints us, we can find substitutes at the click of a mouse. Video games gobble up countless hours of youth, lust engulfs healthy sexual desire, and the anonymity of cyberspace creates the illusion of community and friendship without the real demands of true intimacy. Wherever reality falls short, fantasy promises a quick and painless escape.

Fantasy also exists in the church. Instead of engaging in real discus-sions about the pressing issues and concerns that confront men today, we often accept a caricature of masculinity that bears little resem-blance to the portraits we find in Scripture. Instead of anger, we learn about serenity. Instead of ambition, meekness. Competition gives way to gentleness. Meekness and gentleness aren't wrong, but the church usually presents them in ways that don't help us understand how to be masculine. Often gentleness and meekness come across looking like feminine traits.

The fruit of the spirit sounds lifeless, impossible to enjoy, and so far from how we really live. Instead of a flesh-and-blood Jesus, we get a meek and mild Mr. Rogers. Instead of drunken Noah, lying Abraham, manipulative Jacob, murderous Paul, ambitious John, and competitive Peter, we meet a lineup of saints who always wore a napkin at the dinner table and never passed gas, grew fearful, or complained about how rotten God had treated them. I love that the Bible is often uncom-fortably honest about the people it portrays as saints. If only the church would do the same!

Even in church we settle for the fantasy of masculinity rather than facing and addressing reality. If only we prayed more, led devotions for our families more, or settled for a lower-paying job, we would have it figured out. If only we were more spiritual and less masculine... Many churches propagate this subtle lie.

Men in the church often feel pressured to act more spiritually advanced than they are. Christian men are supposed to be magnificent hus-bands and spiritual leaders. Kevin Leman observes, "Not only are men supposed to attend morning Bible studies, but they're supposed to get home in time for dinner, spend time alone with each child, date their wives once a week, and earn enough money so that their wives can stay home with their young children. This is a heavy load, and some Christian men start to resent it."[1]

We know these demands are not always realistic, but that doesn't stop us from striving to turn "reality as it is" into "reality as I want it to be." I think the Bible calls men to the reverse. The call for men to be strong and courageous is a challenge to engage reality as it is, not as they want it to be. This, I think, is a new definition of courage—one that takes concepts like glory, honor, and duty and places them in the fabric of our well-worn, reality-filled lives. Courage is staying faithful to my wife as she is, not as I wish her to be. Doing my job well as it is, even if it is not what I wish it to be. Loving my friends, my parents, and my kids all in the same way. To be courageous is to resist the sometimes overwhelming temptation to escape, pretend, and fantasize. Don't get me wrong; I've got nothing against the amusements of video technology or the Internet that allow us (in a healthy way) to blow off steam or distract ourselves for a few moments. But I wonder at the effect of it all. I used to think that daydreaming was just the providence of the young; now I am not so sure.

When It Hits the Fan

Because reality rarely lives up to our expectations, we have made a multibillion-dollar industry out of escape. But I am convinced that true masculine courage resists the temptation to avoid reality. Courage isn't only storming the cockpit of an airplane on 9/11, stepping into a gladiator's arena, or charging into battle like William Wallace. All of these are examples of courage, but they stem from the same source: the recognition that life (on whatever level) is out of whack. Real life recognizes that fact.

Courage acknowledges that the plane has been hijacked and is now headed in the wrong direction or that one must fight instead of living in peace and comfort. Courage recognizes that people get sick and die; our kids have minds and wills of their own; and our wives, moms, and girlfriends are far from perfect. And most of all, so am I. Courage embraces the real, even when reality isn't comfortable or convenient. Stepping into this reality isn't glorious or particularly memorable, but it separates the truly brave from the rest of us.

When I was younger, my struggle to find masculinity followed the images I saw in movies. I remember watching *Black Hawk Down* and having a crisis of masculine angst. In the movie, two soldiers tucked away in the safety of a command chopper volunteer to go down to street level and protect a downed pilot against an overwhelming number of enemies. Their act is certain suicide, and yet with dignity, honor, courage, and duty, these men step into that situation. Both are killed while the man they sought to protect is captured but survives the ordeal.

I left the theater wondering if I would have done the same thing. Would I, under such extreme circumstances, react the same way? Or would I hide? I really didn't know. *United Flight 93*, which is about the men and women who attempted to retake a hijacked airliner on 9/11, provoked the same questions. When it counted most, would I do the courageous thing?

I think I may know the answer to those questions now. And I hope you hear this the right way. I would like to *think* that I would. (Whether or not I really *would* is irrelevant to my point here.) If some kind of glory was involved, I think I would put myself in harm's way. But for many of us (who are not military or police, firefighters or missionaries…), our opportunities to be courageous don't look that big and honorable. And that is my point. Biblical courage—true masculine courage—isn't simply doing the glorious thing but also doing the ordinary, mundane, boring, decidedly *inglorious* stuff of life.

I want us to understand that courage isn't only in the big accomplishments. It is in the small acts too, which is where the vast majority of men live, struggling with whether they are truly men.

The problem with looking to Hollywood for the image of true masculinity (even those true-to-life stories of courage) is that it feeds my desire for glory. But when I leave the theater and scratch the car door next to me getting into my car, my decision about whether or not to leave a note admitting my mistake isn't glorious. Nobody will notice what I decide. No one will make a movie about my choice. I can hide if I choose to. Situations like this determine and shape our courage, honor, duty, and virtue.

Or imagine leaving the theater and returning home to a wife who is sexually unresponsive. Or perpetually angry. Or domineering. Or unkempt. The temptation to find release and fulfillment elsewhere can be overwhelming. Escape promises what reality can't provide. Our response in that moment can be just as courageous as what we do when we decide to protect a fallen pilot or storm a cockpit.

Courage is visiting our moms and dads and caring for them as they grow older instead of abandoning them to others' care. Courage is faithfulness to my wife when she isn't all I'd hoped for. Courage is integrity in business when no one else sees it, or refusing to sleep with my girlfriend when she happens to be drunk and willing, or having the tough conversation, or keeping my promise when I'd rather do anything else.

Hollywood doesn't make movies about this true masculine courage.

The Goodness of Thorns

My mind is filled with examples of times when I chose to escape instead of dealing with the difficulties of life. So many times I hid when I needed to step forward, or I withheld love when someone needed it, or I punished when I should have forgiven. I'm going to tell you a story about when I got it right, but I don't want you to get the wrong idea. I often don't. But in this case, my masculine angst led me to God, and by His grace, onward to courage.

My wife and I have a really cool set of kids. They are amazing. And

I have found that I really like being a dad. But one of our kids was diagnosed with a developmental disorder that has a significant stigma attached to it. I remember the exact moment when the weight of this crashed in on me. After months of ignorance and then denial, the diagnosis hit home. I was driving home talking to my wife about it, and I began to sob over the future I was sure this disorder had stolen from my child. I pictured my kid being the one in the corner whom all the others teased. I was disappointed, mad, and overwhelmed with what this meant for our family's future. I know this sounds overly dramatic; our child wasn't dying of cancer or killed in an accident. But for my wife and me, who had dreams of "perfect" kids, it was a huge deal.

At some point later, I had a conversation with a friend who said something I will never forget. He said that I need to love my child as my child is, not as I want my child to be. Reality had bitten, but I could bite back. I did not have to accept this passively and resign myself to lifelong disappointment. I could choose to love and welcome and accept my child as my kid is and not worry about what could have been.

I know these words may sound cliché to you, but in that moment, they changed everything for me. Instead of hiding, escaping, and manipulating, I began to simply be a dad to the children I really have, not to my ideal of what my children should have been.

This choice, by God's grace, has led to many others. Life is still hard and full of twinges of sadness or anger at God or life. But disappointment has given way to delight. Duty to joy. Literal mourning to literal dancing. I wouldn't change a thing. I wouldn't want it to be any different.

Paul had a similar experience. We are not quite sure what his challenge was (some think it could have been a physical issue, others think it was an emotional one), but he writes about it in 2 Corinthians 12:

> I will boast about a man like that, but I will not boast about myself, except about my weaknesses...To keep me from

becoming conceited…there was given me a thorn in my flesh, a messenger of Satan, to torment me. Three times I pleaded with the Lord to take it away form me. But he said to me, "My grace is sufficient for you, for my power is made perfect in weakness." Therefore I will boast all the more gladly about my weaknesses, so that Christ's power may rest on me. That is why, for Christ's sake, I delight in weaknesses, in insults, in hardships, in persecutions, in difficulties. For when I am weak, then I am strong (2 Corinthians 12:5,7-10).

This is the paradox of masculine courage: We are at our best when we are weakest.[2] Our weakness forces us to quit hiding behind our poses and postures (our fig leaves, if you will—more about those later) and to confront reality as it is. Such courage overcomes the self-absorption that infects our souls. I'm convinced that the true opposite of love (which is working for the benefit of another) is selfishness. Selfishness works against love, freedom, and courage, convincing me that my own wants, needs, fears, and preferences come first. It takes God-filled courage to lay those things down for the sake of another.

This way of being male—being at our best when we are weakest—fits perfectly into the upside-down nature of the kingdom of Jesus. If you want to lose your life, try to save it. In order to save your life, you must lose it for the sake of Jesus and His kingdom. If you want to be exalted, be humbled first. If you want to be first, you must be last.

If you want to know the mind of God, just turn everything this world values and believes upside down; then you'll begin to get the idea. So it makes perfect sense that in God's kingdom, men are strongest when they admit weakness. That is real courage. I love how one teacher puts it: "Weak is the new strong."[3]

The only alternative to this authentic way of living is to pretend to be strong when we are not. We can hide and continually run to our areas of strength whenever something threatens to expose us as weak. We hate weakness and humility, but they are the paths to surrender. Learning to live in weakness opens us up to life in this world at its fullest.

Life "how it's supposed to be" fades away, and we become willing to accept life as it really is.

Jesus serves as our model for this. He lived in absolute dependence on the Father. There is mystery in this, but Jesus consistently reminded His disciples that He was only doing what He saw the Father doing and saying what the Father told Him to say.[4] Jesus "did not consider equality with God something to be grasped, but made himself nothing, taking the very nature of a servant, being made in human likeness. And being found in appearance as a man, he humbled himself and became obedient to death—even death on a cross!"[5]

Many of us have been raised to be ashamed of our weakness, dependence, and brokenness. We were told early and often to "quit being such a baby." But we cannot be the strong rescuers of others until we see that we ourselves are in need of rescue. We cannot be strong until we admit that we are not strong. Until we are broken, our lives will be self-serving, self-reliant, and self-absorbed.

Lessons in the Wilderness

Everyone God has used in a great way has learned this lesson. Moses spent 40 years as a no-name shepherd to learn that his strength (which he used to kill an Egyptian who was abusing an Israelite slave) would not bring about Israel's freedom. Forty years! Then God gave Moses a career of doing incredible acts that showcased *God's* power. Paul waited 14 years after his conversion before he began his first missionary journey. Jesus "learned obedience" during the first 30 years of His life before His public ministry began.[6] Joseph and David each endured similar periods of testing and insignificance.

We often forget that this is how God prepares people. We gain true strength when we come at last to the end of our resources and ourselves. Erwin McManus notes this trend in the Bible:

> The history of God's people is not a record of God searching for courageous men and women who would handle the

task, but God transforming the hearts of cowards and calling them to live courageous lives. Adam and Eve hid; Abraham lied; Moses ran; David deceived; Esther was uncertain; Elijah contemplated suicide; John the Baptist doubted; Peter denied; Judas betrayed. And those are just some of the leading characters.[7]

For several years now, I have lived with an embarrassing (to me) struggle with depression and anxiety. Mental illness was something I had always joked about, but during a recovery from a minor surgery I began to live with debilitating panic and crushing depression. I was so ashamed. My wife was pregnant with our first child, working, and pursuing her masters degree, so I was embarrassed to be so needy. My parents were full of love, but they just didn't get it. They, like me, thought this was something I would just snap out of if I had a good talking to. I had just started working at a new church and was desperate to prove myself. All of this contributed to my perfect storm.

The longer this went on, the more ashamed I became. When I had broken my arm as a kid, people signed my cast. When I had to walk on crutches after breaking my leg, people gave me sympathy. But mental illness was something else entirely. (Should people sign my *head?*) How do you tell people you can't preach because you're afraid you'll have a nervous breakdown in front of the church?

My wife was concerned, my parents were worried, and the church wasn't quite sure whom they'd hired. I hated this. It warred against everything I thought being strong was (the respect and affection of women, admiration of my parents, and adoration of others). Instead, I was weak. Needy. And I despised myself because of it.

But again, the fundamental choice of this life presented itself: Would I accept life as it was, or would I escape, pretend, numb, or run? Would I lean into weakness and dependence on God, or would I lean toward posturing and posing to protect my ego? I wish this were a one-time set of alternatives, but I have found that this is the essence of what it means to daily follow Jesus and die to ourselves.

This is the reality of life "under the sun" as the writer of Ecclesiastes describes it. This isn't the life we'd hoped for when we were young; this is life in a fallen and dark world. The reality of life isn't glory, honor, adventure, and passion. Maybe we have tastes of these things, but most of life includes diapers, kids, homework, carpool, lawn work, cubicle life, study, rejection, betrayal, illness, failure, weakness, and brokenness. This is the reality in which we live.

And then we hear even worse news: Those rich, good-looking, talented, famous, and handsome guys who can get any girl in the world are not really satisfied either. So we are caught on both ends: We dream of living a more compelling, adventurous life, but then we find out that even the guys who live that way find it empty.

The call to men who live in the community of Jesus is to live in reality and reject the counterfeits and substitutes that fantasy and escape provide. This requires great and constant courage and is much different from the kind of life of which we have probably dreamed. But the Scriptures assure us that this is the life that is really life. Jesus doesn't promise to immunize us from evil and suffering, nor does He provide an escape. Rather, He promises to help us endure difficulties with hope and joy. I have found this to be true. I still have plenty of dark days and anxious moments, but they are different now that I have come to accept them. They become part of my "new normal," and they are evidences of God's grace and mercy. I can tell you with 100 percent certainty that I have become a better man, husband, father, disciple, and pastor because of this thorn.

No Other Stream

As we try to find out what "redeemed masculinity" is like, we must keep this posture of courageous acceptance and response continually before us. It is the basis of everything else. Life won't work and fit together until this is a reality for us. We will examine three areas of a man's world: his work (his "field"), his sex life (his "bedroom"), and his community of relationships (his "arena"). But all this assumes the most important point: the redefinition of strength. Not running from the real world, but engaging it. I am suggesting a whole new way of approaching life. No more independent living, no more acting as though everything is up to us. No more false contentment, which is what we get when we simply ask less out of life or pretend we want no more than what we have.

Courageously embracing reality is the only way to live in God's kingdom as a man and to taste the life that is truly life.

I'm reminded of a conversation between Jill and the lion, Aslan, in C.S. Lewis' *The Silver Chair*. Jill enters the magical land of Narnia only to find herself overcome with thirst and facing the lion at the edge of a stream.

> "If you're thirsty, you may drink."
>
> They were the first words she had heard since Scrubb [another child who had come into Narnia with Jill] had spoken to her on the edge of the cliff. For a second she stared here and there, wondering who had spoken. The voice said again, "If you are thirsty, come and drink," and of course she remembered what Scrubb had said about animals talking in that other world, and realized that it was the lion speaking. Anyway, she had seen its lips move this time, and the voice was not like a man's. It was deeper, wilder, and stronger; a sort of heavy, golden voice. It did not make her any less frightened than she had been before, but it made her frightened in rather a different way.
>
> "Are you thirsty?" said the Lion.
>
> "I'm *dying* of thirst," said Jill.
>
> "Then drink," said the Lion.
>
> "May I—could I—would you mind going away while I do?" said Jill.
>
> The Lion answered this only by a look and a very low growl.

And as Jill gazed at its motionless bulk, she realized that she might as well have asked the whole mountain to move aside for her convenience.

The delicious rippling noise of the stream was driving her nearly frantic.

"Will you promise not to—do anything to me, if I do come?" said Jill.

"I make no promise," said the Lion.

Jill was so thirsty now that, without noticing it, she had come a step nearer.

"*Do* you eat girls?" she said.

"I have swallowed up girls and boys, women and men, kings and emperors, cities and realms," said the Lion. It didn't say this as if it were boasting, nor as if it were sorry, nor as if it were angry. It just said it.

"I daren't come and drink," said Jill.

"Then you will die of thirst," said the Lion.

"Oh dear!" said Jill, coming another step nearer. "I suppose I must go and look for another stream then."

"There is no other stream," said the Lion.[8]

Part Two

IN THE FIELD

Chapter 3

NAMING THE ANIMALS

In our materialistic culture, work is reduced to a utilitarian function: a means of attaining benefits for *this* world, *this* life, whether material gain or self fulfillment. Work no longer has a transcendent purpose as a means of serving and loving God. No wonder, then, that many are questioning the very meaning of work...This offers Christians a rich opportunity to make the case that work is truly fulfilling only when it is firmly tied to its moral and spiritual moorings. It is time for the church to reclaim this crucial part of life, restoring a biblical understanding of work and economics. A biblical theology of work should be a frequent subject for sermons, just as it was during the Reformation, when establishing one's vocation was considered a crucial element in discipleship.

CHARLES COLSON

We simply can't imagine what life in Eden must have been like. The word *Eden* means "delight." God created men and women to have perfect intimacy with Himself, with creation, and with each other. No sin, guilt, or shame. Nothing to fear or worry about. Because sin had not yet entered the world, everything existed in harmony with everything else. The word *shalom* describes what life was like:

> The webbing together of God, humans, and all creation in justice, fulfillment, and delight is what the Hebrew prophets called *shalom*. We call it "peace" but it means far more than just a peace of mind or cease-fire between enemies...In the Bible, *shalom* means universal flourishing, wholeness, and delight—a rich state of affairs in which natural needs are satisfied and natural gifts fruitfully employed, all under the arch of God's love.[1]

The opening two chapters of Genesis present a normative picture of the way God intended people to live and flourish. "Working" God's creation was a part of this picture. The first commands God gave human beings had to do with work. They were to "rule over the fish of the sea and the birds of the air, over the livestock, over all the earth, and over all the creatures that move along the ground" (Genesis 1:26). God commanded them to "be fruitful and increase in number; fill the earth and subdue it. Rule over the fish of the sea and the birds of the air and over every living creature that moves on the ground" (Genesis 1:28).

In the midst of this sinless world, God gave humanity the mandate to work and to steward creation. This creation mandate consisted of the commands to (1) fill the earth, (2) subdue it, (3) rule over all the animals, and (4) work and take care of the garden. What God had made and declared good, human beings were to cultivate and use to glorify Him and benefit others.

God rules, governs, and creates, so human beings made in His likeness should do the same. God gave creation to the man and the woman to steward and to work. This stewardship is commonly called the *creation mandate*. It is not just a Christian thing; it is a human thing.

What we call *work* is part of what it is to be a human being. Work was not a result of the fall, but God's intention for humanity from the beginning. As we will see shortly, this has radical implications for what it means to be masculine.

These directives describe our mandate to comanage with God the things He has made. He has never rescinded these commands, and because they preceded the fall and entrance of sin and death into the world, we understand that labor is not a consequence of sin. In other words, we would work even if the fall had never occurred. Working with God is part of what it means to be human. Work is a way we imitate what God is like. We work because He works (Genesis 2:2 says that God Himself labored to fashion our world during the six days of creation). God made us in His image, and this means we too live in the rhythms of speech and silence, work and rest.

All of this also suggests that God did not create a static world.[2] He commanded us to direct it and take it somewhere. It was good, but not complete; there was more to be done. God created things that have the ability to create other things—to cultivate, design, build, grow, and learn to use the resources of creation to benefit others. This is holy work. Planting flowers, tending soil, knitting sweaters, pounding metals—all of this reflects the fact that God made us in His image. To sin is to take the creation in a direction that God doesn't want it to go or to do nothing with it at all.

Even thousands of years later, this is still part of what it means to be human and to be made in God's image. All of our good, creative, and directive pursuits flow from Genesis 1–2. Now we understand that when we work and care for the world, we express worship, we are more fully human, and we reflect what God is like. Again, the Bible doesn't start in Genesis 3: Creation isn't bad, work isn't a result of sin, and being human is still a good thing. Yes, all of these things have been stained with sin and fallenness, but that isn't the whole story. Creation is bursting with life and potential, and people are placed in the middle of it to work it and care for it. To subdue the earth does not mean to pillage and strip-mine it but rather to direct it in ways that glorify God and benefit other human beings.

We were given the task to order, manage, and develop God's wonderful creation and to bring to light all the potential hidden within it. Before sin entered the world, God commanded that we do this, and it was part of His good design for human beings.

This doesn't mean, of course, that we are on our own, as if it were all up to us. God is sovereign, and He is directing all things for the ultimate good of His people (Romans 8:28) and His glory (Romans 11:33-36). God is still active in creation, holding it together (Colossians 1:17) and sustaining all things (Hebrews 1:3). "Man as the image bearer is somehow involved in the shaping of the history that God ultimately controls."[3]

God uses our wills and our freedom to bring about His ends. He can even use someone or something that is opposed to Him to bring about His will (Paul gives several examples of this in Romans 9). We are not simply actors who are following a script on a cosmic stage, nor are we playwrights who write the story by themselves. We fall somewhere in between. We are graced with the dignity of stewardship and co-regency, yet we are humbly dependent on God for our very breath.

God gave us the power, out of the rich potential He embedded in creation, to bring about the world of our choosing. Of course, God is the author of all things. We have done nothing to earn this honor; He has given it to us as an act of grace. We deserve no credit for the work we do, for all things belong to Him.[4]

In other words, God gave Adam and Eve work to do. God's creation was good, but that didn't mean it would care for itself. God certainly could have done a better job managing the earth than we have, but for many reasons, He gave us the privilege of being co-stewards with Him as together we govern creation. So God creates the universe and nestles the man in the Garden of Eden, and He then turns His good creation over to Adam (and all human beings).

Work and Rest

In Genesis 2:5 *Adam* is created from the *adamah*, the ground. The wordplay between *Adam* and *adamah* is intentional. On one hand it affirms Adam's intimate association with the dust of the earth and thereby humanity's physical nature. On the other hand, it prepares the reader for the man's responsibility to take care of the garden.

Let's look at each of the commands of the creation mandate in a little more detail.

Filling the earth is the task of enjoying all of it, not just one part. We are also to rule over the earth. We rule by having dominion over the animals who inhabit creation and by subduing the land for our purposes and benefit. We rule as co-regents of the Creator, bringing the whole earth under human auspices so we may in turn glorify God with it. Our authority, however, is derived from God's authority, and we are ultimately subject to Him as His creatures.

We were called to work the garden and care for it. The human race was to spread out over all the earth, so we can reasonably conclude that the instructions about the garden were to apply to the whole earth also. *Abad,* the Hebrew word that we translate *work,* is close to the concept of worship or service. When people worked the earth, they were at the same time serving and worshipping their creator.

The final command was to keep the garden. The Hebrew word is *shamar,* which means to exercise great care over, or to guard something of value from an external enemy. The same term is usually translated *keep* in the Aaronic benediction of Numbers 6:24 and describes the way God tenderly guards and looks out for His people. Even after the fall, the vital relationship between humans and the creation around them remains a central part of being human.

The point for our purposes is this: Man has a special relationship to the earth; our *imagio dei* is linked forever to our role as caretaker and steward. The man, *adam,* comes from the ground, *adamah,* but *adam* is to work and tend to the *adamah.* Working the earth and being masculine (and fully human) cannot be separated.

Pushing creation forward, directing, arranging, managing, and creating are all fundamental features of being human and of being masculine. This means that the general activity of work (not our specific vocation, which we may hate) make us human in a way nothing else does. As others have said, more than a paycheck is lost when someone

becomes unemployed. God means for us to spend our days expend-
ing ourselves by tending the earth.

Something is God-honoring in this as well. We have seen that the
Hebrew word for work, *abad,* is also translated as *serve* or *worship.*
The Old Testament concept of work and worship are related. Humanity's call to work the ground is crucial for understanding the world and
our place in it. We bring God glory when we reenact His creating,
ordering, and directing activity. The New Testament tells us, "Whatever
you do, whether in word or deed, do it all in the name of the Lord
Jesus, giving thanks to God the Father through him."[5] Because we are
spiritual beings, we can direct anything we do toward the glory of
God as worship.

This is not to say that our work should be all-consuming. Immediately
after creating human beings on the sixth day, God rested.

> By the seventh day God had finished the work he had been
> doing; so on the seventh day he rested from all his work. And
> God blessed the seventh day and made it holy, because on it
> he rested from all the work of creating he had done (Genesis
> 2:2-3).

This rest forms the basis of the Sabbath commands (to rest and to
refrain from work one day a week) that are developed later in the
Hebrew Bible. Our work is important, but it's not indispensable. Keeping the Sabbath was a way to remember this balance. We act as
God acted in the rhythm of work and rest. The rest ensures we take
time to remember God and worship Him, refresh our bodies and
souls, and fight against the temptation to be defined by what we do.
Regardless of whether you think the Sabbath commands are for New
Testament believers today, they represent great wisdom. To find significance, identity, value, and worth beyond our work remains a difficult
challenge for most men.

Regardless of our specific jobs, we must find our work within this
greater story. Far too many of us understand what we do as simple
provision—for our families or for disposable income to enjoy on the

weekends—and we miss the greater picture. To be fully masculine is to engage the world as God's stewards in order to direct creation for the benefit of others. Many workers—doctors, farmers, teachers, and chemists, for example—easily sense this stewardship. It's essentially built into their jobs. But others, like mortgage brokers, telemarketers, and used-car salesmen, may have a harder time defining how their work benefits God, others, and creation itself.

From Ants to Zebras

One of man's assignments was to name all the animals that God had created. To name something in the ancient world was a huge deal. To appreciate this, think of the tremendous difference between calling people by their name or by their title. I have many titles: pastor, husband, friend, son, brother, father, taxpayer...But my wife never calls me those (unless she wants to point out what a dork I am when I get mad at someone while I am driving. "Nice job, *Pastor*"). Instead, she calls me Mike. How ridiculous would it be for her to call me, "fellow American citizen"?

Names (and naming) have great significance in the Scriptures. In the ancient world, a name was more than just what someone called you; in some ways, it revealed who you were. The Israelites named places for what had happened there, and they named children for how they were born (Jacob), what they looked like (Esau), or what their parents hoped they would be.

When God did a great work in somebody, He often changed his or her name (Abram became Abraham, and Jacob became Israel). This meant more than just simply calling them something else; it represented a change in their identity. Again, names were a big deal. The moment when God revealed His name to Moses in Exodus chapter 3 could not have been more significant. Praying in Jesus' name means more than just adding a tag line; it is praying on behalf of Jesus, praying as Jesus would pray.

Knowing all this about names and naming, I find it interesting that God gave Adam the task of naming the animals. God brought the animals to him to see what he would name them. Naming the animals was an expression of Adam's stewardship over them and his responsibility to them. "To name something implied the authority to define its character, to give shape to its nature, to fill a void with something that came out of the one who gave the name."[6]

This raises many questions. Adam was just a clump of dirt a few verses back. Why is God handing His creation over to him? He didn't have any previous experience with this or some unique skill that God lacked. Obviously, God didn't need Adam's help, but He desired it nonetheless. This is significant. We can't know for sure why God does this. Perhaps He is so full of joy that He can't help but invite someone else into it. Perhaps He made us to reflect Him as miniature versions of Him—working, governing, and creating. Whatever the reasons, God could have done it alone and done it better, but instead He invited Adam into the partnering process. Adam named things, and in doing so, he connected himself to them.

Men still do this work today. We may not literally name the animals, but we nevertheless exercise dominion over creation in partnership with God in a similar fashion. The fact that we also have a capacity to make moral choices as we "name the animals" today means that we too can choose to direct creation in ways that are God-honoring and beneficial. Or we can use our gifts to pillage and plunder creation for our own selfish ends, as we see happening countless times in our world today. As a whole, humanity has failed to see that we can develop God's creation around us *and* preserve it at the same time. Instead, we have exploited what God has made and have used it for our short-term benefit with little or no thought for the long-term consequences of our actions.

This temptation shows itself immediately back in Genesis 3. Cain, one of the sons of Adam and Eve, worked the fields, while his brother, Abel, kept flocks of sheep. Both begin to create and arrange and work with all the stuff God has given to them. But conflict erupts between them because they fail to link their work properly to their relationship with God.

The question for men is always this: Will we use what God has given us in harmony with His intent to make the world better? Will we cooperate with God, using what we have and do to effect His purposes ("your kingdom come") and to advance His desires on the earth ("your will be done")?

We face this question today. Have we used computers to step beyond what God would want for His people? How about the technology behind television? What about our knowledge of chemistry, physics, and biology, which we use for medicine but also for weaponry? The same is true with all created things: We can use them for God's purposes or against them. Sexuality, food, our bodies—all can be used for good or evil. Our struggle with the way we use our stuff began in Genesis.

Creation is moving. It is not static. It will go somewhere, and we are called to steward it. We can't help but live in intimate interaction with creation, and we are called to arrange and guide it according to God's purposes for it. When we see pictures of oil spills or clear-cut rain forests, we can't help but feel that something has been violated. We stand at the beach or in the middle of Yosemite National Park, and we cannot help but think of the damage we have worked and are capable of working against creation. We are not called to worship creation, but to take care of it. God gave humans responsible dominion over the created world, and He gives each of us smaller, more limited kingdoms where we can have our say. We get to direct creation to suit our wants and needs. Not as owners, but as stewards—those who care for someone else's property. This mandate is not restricted to the direct acts of planting, sowing, building, and gardening. It includes all of our cultural endeavors: government, education, justice, art, and family. As Cornelius Plantinga has said, "Human beings are charged not only to care for the earth and animals (subduing what is already there), but also to develop certain cultural possibilities (filling out what is only potentially there)."[7]

God can use anyone or anything to sovereignly fulfill His purposes, including those who are opposed to Him. Because of the common grace of God, many people who don't know or follow Jesus may still lead the way in caring for the earth.[8] Of course, we disagree with those who see humanity as a blight on the world or who understand every part of creation to be part of God, but we admit that some people who are outside the kingdom want to see *shalom* and justice and that they work toward it, consciously or not. A person does not have to believe in Christ in order to do Christ's work in the world.

Genesis 1–2 also suggests that our modern separation of spiritual work and nonspiritual work is completely false. The Hebrew language has no word for *spiritual* because that would imply that some things are not. The same is true with our work. We don't have to label it *Christian* or *spiritual* for it to be holy and sacred. The impulse to work that God has placed inside us has little to do with church or religious work. We need to understand that the impulse behind most of our labor has its roots in this creation mandate. Medicine? Using the resources of the created world to benefit others. Law? Bringing justice and harmony to the way people relate to each other. Politics? Helping people organize themselves to bring about the most good for the most people. All of these vocations can be abused, of course, but these are all ways we can partner with God to move creation forward. This does not mean putting a Christian label on them. Sometimes we ruin what we do by labeling it.

Where does your job fit into this picture? How does what you do enable you or others to exercise dominion over the earth, cultivating its resources for the benefit of human beings? If you can see how your occupation fits in that process, you will discover a divine nobility to your tasks. God meets us as much in the daily grind as He does in the religious and spectacular.

Men shouldn't work only because we need money or for the chance to enjoy ourselves in the evenings and on the weekends. Maybe that is why we have the particular job we do, but that is not why we work.

We work because something about it fulfills our humanity. As the retired and the unemployed will attest, we lose more than money when the daily rhythm of employment is interrupted.[9]

Many men today work simply to make money. The "naming the animals" impulse from Genesis 2 has been lost or diminished in the pursuit of a dollar. But then what? What about leaving the world better than you found it or inventing something new and useful? These interests are swallowed up by our desire for financial security. But this doesn't satisfy our primal longing to do something more. It leaves us empty and shallow. Is this really what we want to do with our one chance at life? Work is not just about paying our bills; it is about making a contribution to life, others, and history.

I love Richard Rohr's warning about money:

> Money is an empty symbol precisely because it stands for anything and everything besides the paper or metal it is made of. It stands for me and my importance. Money has no inherent meaning, which is why it can hold any false meaning that we want to put on it. Besides this, the paper and metal are practically worthless. This then is why directing one's life toward the making of money is so dangerous. It is a commitment to making what is inherently meaningless and worthless, yet onto it we project all sorts of value and importance.[10]

It is far too easy to fall in love with money and to lose the spiritual nature of our work. If we do not explicitly dethrone money, it will not stay a neutral force in our lives. It *will* demand our allegiance.

> We make a great deal of the Ten Commandments, yet I wonder if you have ever heard a single sermon in your life on the tenth commandment? As a Catholic, I never have. It is the very name of the main game and would never occur to us as a problem, much less a sin. "Coveting our neighbors' goods" is now called shopping, advertising and contributing to the gross national product (GNP) and the American economy.

Amazing how the capital sin of greed can be transmuted into a major virtue.[11]

We have so much creative work to do in the world—so much caretaking and filling and stewarding—we'll never run out of wonderful ways to exercise dominion through our culture-making endeavors.[12] Making money should only be a secondary concern.

Even the American ideal of retirement reflects a self-interested, materialistic bias. The Bible never encourages a stage of life where we are independent enough to simply do what we want to do. Many men do use retirement as an opportunity to give and serve. But more often than not, retirement becomes an excuse for indulgence. Maybe we think we've earned the right to do absolutely nothing because we've worked for years at a job we've hated. Or maybe we just want to try new things. Either way, if we focus exclusively on our pursuits and ourselves, something starts to die within us. This is the stage of life when the community around us needs us the most. The younger generations need those at this stage to be more active, more involved, and more willing to serve as spiritual mentors and fathers.

We must find more meaning to our work and rest.

> All of us may offer our gifts and energies to the cause of God's program in the world. When we make this offering by means of an ordinary occupation, we will sometimes feel as if our lives are very ordinary. No matter. An ordinary occupation done conscientiously builds the kingdom of God. Jesus built the kingdom as a carpenter before he built it as a rabbi. And he taught us in the parable of the talents that the question for disciples is not which callings they have but how faithfully they will pursue them.[13]

To serve Jesus as men requires that we remain active in situations that promote the interests of the kingdom (whether they readily appear to or not). Having a job and going to work is one way we do that. But of course, the biblical sense of work is much larger. Voting, paying taxes, obeying laws, and raising children are all ways we bring glory and honor to God (and find meaning and purpose) through work. The key to this is understanding that our efforts should be others-centered. Not just for my benefit, but for others. To love in God's world that way is to "name the animals."

Chapter 4

TOIL AND THORNS

The truth is that nothing in this earth can finally satisfy us. Much can make us content for a time, but nothing can fill us to the brim. The word for this recognition is *longing*...everybody knows there is something about human life that is out of line or out of whack. We can be happy at times, but not totally fulfilled. Even when we have happiness, we fear we'll lose it. Worse, every day brings us fresh news of old evils—nature ravaged, God blasphemed, people cheated, battered, terrorized. Hope is the reach of our hearts for the cure. It's the reach of our hearts toward what we think will fulfill us, secure us, save us—and not just us, but also the whole world.

CORNELIUS PLANTINGA JR.

Although Genesis 1–2 describes God's intention for the world, we live in the reality of Genesis 3. God created us to experience peace and rest (*shalom*) in His good creation. He intended human beings to live in harmony with Him, each other, and the rest of the created order. Man's relationships, sexuality, and work (stewardship) all fit into that design.

Bent Toward the Ground

We'll look at Adam and Eve's disobedience more closely in later chapters, but for now we want to take note of what God did in response to their sin. God immediately pronounces curses on the serpent and the ground as well as judgments on the woman and the man.

> So the LORD God said to the serpent, "Because you have done this, cursed are you above all the livestock and all the wild animals! You will crawl on your belly and you will eat dust all the days of your life. And I will put enmity between you and the woman, and between your offspring and hers; he will crush your head, and you will strike his heel" (Genesis 3:14-15).

This passage signals the beginning of a war on the earth. Two kingdoms vie for the allegiance of human hearts: the kingdom of darkness and death, characterized by the serpent, and the kingdom of God, promised in the coming of a Savior. Notice the offer of hope implicit in this verse. Somehow the serpent will produce offspring (representing the growth of evil over the earth). But from the woman's offspring will come one who will destroy this evil even while being affected by it Himself. Of course, many Christians see this as the first promise of the coming of the Messiah, Jesus, who fulfilled this promise, destroying evil by experiencing the very worst it could offer.[1] So God immediately promises that the state of affairs introduced in Genesis 3 will not continue forever. He was already at work in response to it.

God then turns His attention from the serpent to Eve:

> To the woman he said, "I will greatly increase your pains in childbearing; with pain you will give birth to children. Your desire will be for your husband, and he will rule over you" (Genesis 3:16).

What God says to the woman has great significance for our understanding of masculinity. That discussion will wait a few chapters, but for now we see that God's judgment of Eve will affect her call (to fill the earth and multiply), and also her relationship to her husband. As a result of the fall, men and women and husbands and wives will experience less trust, intimacy, and delight and more power struggles in their relationships.[2] The man will struggle with issues of power, control, and manipulation. He will exploit the woman's desire for him for his own benefit. (For instance, why else would so many women starve themselves to be thin?)

She, on the other hand, will be yearning for him to be something he can never be. He can never, under the judgments of Genesis 3, fulfill the woman the way he was intended to in God's original design. She will always want more out of him, and he will begin to resent her demands.

> To Adam he said, "Because you listened to your wife and ate from the tree about which I commanded you, 'You must not eat of it,' cursed is the ground because of you; through painful toil you will eat of it all the days of your life. It will produce thorns and thistles for you, and you will eat the plants of the field. By the sweat of your brow you will eat your food until you return to the ground, since from it you were taken; for dust you are and to dust you will return" (Genesis 3:17-19).

This passage is the key to understanding the current state of masculinity. It is the reason for so many books on the subject, and it reveals why so many of us resonate with Luke Skywalker moments of yearning.

Much of modern Christianity actually softens, tames, and apologizes for God. We try to reduce His mysteries into 30-second "Bible answer man" sound bites, we avoid the passages in the Bible that make us squeamish and uncomfortable, and we let God off the hook for things for which He accepts full responsibility.

For example, we try to pin gender confusion and masculine struggle on the church, the women's movement, or the media. These all may play a part, but Genesis 3 couldn't be clearer: God is the author of the masculine condition. He is the reason men will never reach that point where we just sit back and say, "Life couldn't be better; I've got it all figured out." God's judgment on the man created an environment where life would not work well; we would never fully arrive or completely answer the questions that haunt the souls of most men. And the ground is cursed—it has been removed from God's blessing or favor. It is no longer under His protection, and so it now works against the purpose for which it was designed.

Notice that the good work of Genesis 1–2 (including stewarding, caring, and protecting) now becomes painful toil. The curse isn't *that* we work but that our work will no longer go smoothly. No longer will the rest of God's creation cooperate with our efforts to direct and steward it.[3] Instead of enjoying a nurturing and peaceful environment, we must be on guard against it. Try not mowing your backyard for a month and see what happens, or watch the *Animals Gone Wild* television shows that highlight the ways animals display aggression toward human beings. We know that creation is set against us.

The *imago dei* in humanity was not destroyed at the fall, but it was greatly disfigured. Men and women continue to fulfill their cultural mandate, but now their decisions and actions are twisted toward self-glory and self-satisfaction.

But something even deeper is at work here. God ties much of our identity to naming animals and working the soil as we govern creation with Him. Then God strikes men where they are most vulnerable by cursing the work men are to do. *Work* becomes *toil,* and this undermines men's sense of significance and identity. By creating an environment where life no longer works well, God thwarts our God-designed need to find significance in what we do. Work is no longer easy, so neither is masculinity. We struggle to find purpose and meaning. Most of us hate our jobs. Most of us are (in our natural, primal, and post-fall state) in conflict with our wives (more about that later). And we continually feel inadequate for all the things we feel compelled to do.

Many men's bosses become their gods. We line up authority figures and attempt to earn their approval in order to answer the nagging doubts that we aren't really men. We place our God-ordained needs for worth, significance, and purpose in others' hands. We crave their validation. We try to fulfill these base-level needs through what we do. Men always ask each other, "What do you do?" because what we do shapes and defines us in ways we don't always understand. We are looking for who we are as men in what we do. Our lives are based on work, earning, and performance. No wonder we are confused when we show up at church and hear about God's free gift of grace to us.

God has set us up. He designed us to work and be in relationship. He then frustrates our attempts to make life work and find significance in our work. He exposes our inadequacy and our vulnerability. Instead of directing, arranging, and creating with joy and confidence, we spend most of our adult lives trying to understand what it means to be a man, only to realize we'll never really live up to the ideal. Or even worse, we realize that the ideal itself is not really the ideal at all.

As we have seen, God's judgment wasn't that Adam had to work, but that God Himself would frustrate his work. God introduced a struggle into creation that dogged Adam as he worked in the world. God strikes men where it hurts most: in the field. He frustrates our labor, our strength—our most vulnerable spot because that's where we derive our self-worth. Every man now experiences the frustration of futility and failure; regardless of how much a man achieves, it is never enough. Money, sex, accomplishment, acclaim, status, possessions...nothing will quench the thirst of the masculine soul. We always need more. We are only as good as our last deal, our last game, our last sermon, or our last date. Our worst fear becomes the fear of never measuring up.

God, Puzzles, and You

If God sometimes seems to be working against us, it's because He is. This is the key to understanding what masculinity looks like outside of Eden. This is the central point that begins our discovery for what it means to live as a man in the middle of this fallen world. It all starts here. God frustrates the things the man wants most. And this is the second-most important point: He does this as an act of mercy!

These judgments were merciful because God ensured that we cannot possibly make life work apart from Him. God introduced problems into the very core of masculinity (and femininity) in order to drive us back to Himself. I love this quote: "Until a man knows he is a man, he will forever go on trying to prove he is one."[4]

I have attempted one jigsaw puzzle in my life. As a pastor, I often suffer from the Monday morning blues. After preaching four weekend services, I wake up Monday tired and depressed. Nothing sounds fun or refreshing. During one particularly dreary Monday, I decided to go buy a puzzle. Strangely enough, I thought it would help me relax. Even more embarrassingly, I picked a 750-piece Thomas Kincaid puzzle that was full of flowers and pastels. (As I said, I wasn't myself that day!) I spent three days on it before throwing it into the trash (along with the idea that puzzles are somehow relaxing). But I learned several lessons. The most important parts of the puzzle are not the flat-sided edge pieces or even the corner pieces. The most important part of the puzzle is the cover of the puzzle box that shows you how the dumb thing will look if you ever put it together.

Genesis 3 is God's way of creating a puzzle, designing men with an insatiable need to put it together, and then hiding the box top so we can't see what it is supposed to look like. Or better yet, Genesis 3 is God's way of declaring Himself to be the box top; no other way of putting the puzzle together will work. This is an act of His grace and mercy. God knew that if life worked well on its own and men could find significance, purpose, and meaning apart from Him, we would. So, as an act of severe kindness, He drives us back to Himself by making life difficult.

We Are Vulnerable

Our struggle in life does two things.[5] First, it heightens our vulnerability and exposes our thirst for more by constantly reminding us we are not in control of life. Most of us, whether we know it or not, try to find our way back to Eden. We spend all of our time and energy searching for *shalom*, intimacy, significance, and rest. Most of the time, we use some form of technology to bring this about. But technological advances won't prevent our bodies from eventually wearing out, and we will all die. Smaller cell phones and larger and flatter televisions will never free us from the gnawing realization that these things are only distractions that keep up the illusion of control and safety. Try as we might to find rest and fulfillment, we will be frustrated at every turn. Anyone who does his own yard work knows this! We will never come to a place where we have nothing to worry about, nothing to fix, and nothing begging us for attention. We are restless, and that restlessness is built into us and into this life. We'll never be fully satisfied with life.

How many athletes, rock stars, movie stars, or other famous people have commented on the emptiness of fame and fortune? How many celebrity divorces does it take to actually convince us that perfect bodies and (alleged) great sex do not make a real, lasting relationship? How many times must we see someone else crash and burn before we wonder if it could happen to us?

For all our exercise, nutrition, and medicine, we still get physically and emotionally sick. For all our leisure time and disposable income, we still grow bored. Is the good life working at a job we tolerate for 40 years (taking two weeks' vacation per year) and then retiring to some gated community to spend our time complaining about the neighbors or the weather? For all of our thinking, striving, motivating, and working, life still won't work. This simple fact exposes us for what we really are: small, fragile creatures who are immensely frightened of our own mortality. God drives us back to Him by reminding us of this constantly.

Anger is usually our natural response to this state of affairs. I work (whether I know it or not) to find my way back to Eden, only to be frustrated at every turn. Much of the anger we experience is rooted in this attempt to bring control and peace to our world. How else can we explain the explosion of road rage and seemingly mindless violence expressed over the smallest of things? Isn't this indicative of how frustrated by the Creator we really are?

Hunger and Thirst

The curses of Genesis 3 are also designed to lead us back to our hunger and thirst for something more. Deep down, we know that right and wrong, good and evil exist side by side. We hate having things stolen from us, seeing our loved ones hurt or abused, or watching someone cheat us out of something we feel belongs to us. An inner primal cry rises from every one of us that this is not the way it should be! We long for freedom, security, intimacy, meaning, significance, and love. All of our art, drama, music, and poetry attest to these things.

What we learn about God from this passage is significant. We learn that He is free and untamed and good. Relentlessly so. He will use anything to draw us back to Himself. Most of us are threatened by the wild, untamed God of the Old Testament, so we tame Him, relegate Him to being just the God of Israel, or spend our time apologizing for the ways in which He seems a little politically incorrect. In truth, such a God threatens us. We feel threatened because He takes away all our power to control or engineer the life we want. We are ultimately powerless over most of our lives, and the masculine virtues of performance and achievement give way to surrender, weakness, and trust.[6] Genesis 3 reminds us that we cannot control God at all, not even through our religious performance. The whole masculine journey starts from this point, where we are called to vulnerably trust in God rather than trusting our own worth or deservedness.

Work and Worship

So the judgments of Genesis 3 show God's mercy. I have talked to so many men (and have been one myself) who have admitted that if not for struggle, adversity, or trial, they wouldn't have come to Jesus. Many think that such an admission is an act of weakness. That is *exactly* what it is. And all of life is designed to bring us to this point. The moment we surrender control (or the perceived illusion of it), we find ourselves in the barren wild of God's ruthless love. At precisely that point of risk, when we no longer have it in ourselves to impress God or others, we realize we just can't make life work through our own effort and resources, and we discover the freedom and courage that defines true men.

If my own strength, power, resources, and nature were sufficient for me to carve out a meaningful and happy life without any help, I would. In an instant. That is the essence of sin: I want to be god, to call the shots, to direct my life. But God, in His mercy, relentlessly keeps this from happening.

The rest of the Bible is the story of the choices people have made (good and bad, from which we get to learn) to handle this difficulty. In response to pain and adversity, we will turn to *something*. And we have only two choices: to worship a part of creation or to worship the Creator.[7] That's it.

Worship isn't a religious word; it is a human word. To give our lives to something bigger than us is as much a part of human nature as breathing. We can't help it. There are no exemptions. Every human being on earth worships something. Atheists worship. So do agnostics. So do anarchists and Christians.

The question is, what is the object of our worship? Most of us deal with difficulty (reality) by turning to an aspect of creation for anesthesia; we numb our pain, distract ourselves from it, immerse ourselves in pleasure and indulgence. Porn provides relief from loneliness, insecurity, or lack of sexual fire with our wives. Money props our fragile egos, which are always being called into question. Status or accomplishment relieves us from the masculine condition that haunts us all. We might worship a thing: a car, a job, or a Super Bowl ring. Or a lifestyle: independent, wealthy, married, autonomous. Or a person: movie star, porn star, girl in class. Or perhaps most often, the person I am tempted to worship is me.

The point—and the problem—is that if we turn to something other than the Creator for fulfillment, it will never satisfy or deliver what it promises. This idolatry doesn't have to be dramatic to numb our pain. Most of us simply whittle away at life doing things that are momentarily amusing or important but that have little lasting value.

For those of us who are somehow getting in touch with our vulnerability and thirst, the one true God beckons us toward true masculinity by first stripping away anything else we could be tempted to trust. I have heard people say, "God must take away the little heavens we create so that we hunger for the real thing." He knows us. He knows our vulnerabilities. And this is where He sabotages us—in our labor, our strength, and our success—to drive us back to Himself.

Ruthless Brokenness

We spend most of our lives trying to end-run the curses and judgements of Genesis 3. We look for formulas (If I pray every day for my kid, he'll turn out okay. If I tithe to the church, we'll always have enough money. If I don't have sex before marriage, I'll have a great sex life once the marriage starts) and are swayed by the self-help stuff recycled through the generations. But the curses guarantee that I cannot arrange for the life I desire. The judgments thwart the formulas I might use to deal with the areas of life that matter most (though of course praying, tithing, and waiting until marriage for sex are good things!).

God made life this way on purpose, not to keep us from Himself but to call us back home. He made us for more than this world can offer. The temptation of our hearts is to find satisfaction in the small, fragile joys of this life. God reminds us there is more for us to find.

The words of Larry Crabb are fitting: "Our view of spiritual manhood has more to do with continuing to function in spite of difficulties than with successfully overcoming them. We don't believe the Bible provides a plan for making life work as we think it should. We think it offers a reason to keep on going even when life doesn't work that way."[8]

This doesn't mean we are passive and resigned to accept whatever comes our way. We are called to discern and fight and cry out to God for healing, forgiveness, and freedom. But it does mean that no amount of prayer, religious deeds, or good behavior will ever insulate us fully from the reality of the fallen world around us.

Yes, in our hearts we tend to worship and lean on other things to anesthetize ourselves against the pain of reality. This is the choice before us: We can deaden ourselves through addiction. Attempt to impose our own will on creation through money or power. Distract. Numb. Pretend. Or we can begin our journey into true manhood by allowing our desire for more to lead us to Jesus Christ. The judgments of Genesis 3 either tempt us to hide or they empower us to come out from hiding. We have no other option.

Jesus' interaction with the Samaritan woman in John 4 is a case study in God's genius. Five husbands had set her aside. Jesus acknowledges her brokenness and thirst for more by playfully offering living water so she would never thirst again. He turns her desire for relationship back on itself and points out that what she really thirsts for is Him. Here, and in other places throughout the Bible, God uses the desires of our hearts to lead us back to Him.

We think we can make life fulfill us, but as the writer of Ecclesiastes said, "[God has] set eternity in the hearts of men; yet they cannot fathom what God has done from beginning to end."⁹ God has set us up to be discontent. Our struggle is from Him. He does not allow us to find completeness in this life. We may numb or run or deny or sin, but our desires will always awaken something within us for more out of life. This is the way it should be. The worst thing that could happen to us would be to get used to the idea that this is all there is. No, there is more. And yes, we are missing it. And that leads us right to the very heart of God.

Genesis 3 calls us to turn from our independence (or at least the illusion of it) and live in humble dependence as people who thirst for more than this life can provide. If we understand spiritual growth as the journey from illusion (about self and God) to reality (about self and God), then these judgments make it difficult not to grow toward God. By decreeing that nothing in this world can satisfy us, God arranged human life so that we do nothing but search for what can satisfy. As St. Augustine said, "Our hearts are restless until they find their rest in You."

Chapter 5

HARPS, CLOUDS, AND BACKHOES

To affirm and bask in the goodness of the world, to praise God for the wonders of creation, to practice responsible stewardship of this small planet, and to honor its Maker by using its resources wisely for the welfare of the race and the enriching of human life are all integral aspects of the work that Christians are called to do. Any idea that consistent Christianity must undermine or diminish concern for the tasks of civilization should be dismissed once and for all.

J.I. PACKER

I have a friend who works in the mortgage industry. He does well for himself and doesn't hate his job. But he wonders if this is what he was made for. Is this the adventure that John Eldredge talks about in his book *Wild at Heart*? Sitting in an air-conditioned cubicle from nine to five each day with a half-hour lunch and two weeks of vacation a year? How does someone like this find worth, meaning, and significance in what he does every day? Work for most men is either a source of income or a way of arranging for a life of comfort and indulgence. Is there more to it than that?

Suppose that this man's family needs him to keep the job he has. He doesn't have the luxury of opting for something that more naturally fits into his passions and interests. What do we say to him? Does he just miss out on the masculine journey? Is he somehow diminished because he hasn't found work that he finds satisfying?

How should my friend see his job? As simply a means of paying the bills? Or as something much more?

The first thing we might say to this friend is that he must see his job within the big, epic story we talked about in chapter 3. It is good that he works. It is part of his being human and being a man. And he must find a way to name the animals in his current occupation in order for him to see its place within the larger story. This is absolutely critical if he is to discover God's purposes for him in his job. How does he do this?

We might begin by saying that human beings need shelter. That is not optional. Owning a house, then, is a good thing. Helping people to live in a way that brings comfort and security is an important thing. Not only that, but because of the legal and financial gymnastics involved in buying a home, my friend is offering a valuable service to his clients by guiding them through the bewildering maze of numbers, points, and payments.

This man also does his work with honesty and integrity. He genuinely seems to put his clients first and tries to bring Jesus glory by speaking kindly and considerately to all around him. He truly does his work "as unto the Lord." Is this not worship? Is this any less spiritual than pastoral work or missionary work? Of course not. Many have come to faith because of this man's life and work. He demonstrates what Jesus is like through his kindness and honesty. And he is generous with his money. He works to remedy injustice around him, and he supports several ministries as well as his local church.

Heaven Is a Place on Earth

The final reason that his work is sacred and honorable is this: It is preparing him for what he will do forever in heaven. Sounds crazy, doesn't it? But it's true, and it's what the Scriptures teach.

Let's think about this. What images do you have of heaven? For me, heaven conjures eternal worship services, clouds, harps, and streets of gold. After my whole life is played in front of God and everybody, I get a mansion the same size as everyone else's, and I get to "enjoy" some sort of disembodied, floaty existence while I learn to play the harp and zip around the universe. I'm sure I'll enjoy it (and it *is* better than the other place), but to be honest, this description sounds kind of unreal and boring. Somehow all our talk of singing, feasting, and floating forever doesn't compare with the flesh-and-blood world we find ourselves in.

Fortunately, none of this imagery is correct. Heaven is much more earthly than this.[1]

Heaven is usually the word we use for the place we go when we die. But the Bible teaches something much different. Heaven will be God dwelling on a renewed earth with His people, who have new, resurrected bodies. That is the end of the story. Heaven turns out to be returning to a new earth with new bodies, living with God forever as His people.

Remember, we were created for Eden. And Jesus comes to do more than simply forgive sins.[2] When describing His second coming, Jesus talks of the "renewal of all things":

> I tell you the truth, at the renewal of all things, when the Son of Man sits on his glorious throne, you who have followed me will also sit on twelve thrones, judging the twelve tribes of Israel. And everyone who has left houses or brothers or sisters or father or mother or children or fields for my sake will receive a hundred times as much and will inherit eternal life (Matthew 19:28-29).

Paul says this about Jesus:

> For God was pleased to have all his fullness dwell in him, and
> through him to reconcile to himself all things, whether things on
> earth or things in heaven, by making peace through his blood,
> shed on the cross (Colossians 1:19-20).

Peter presents a similar idea when concluding a sermon:

> Repent, then, and turn to God, so that your sins may be wiped
> out, that times of refreshing may come from the Lord, and that
> he may send the Christ, who has been appointed for you—
> even Jesus. He must remain in heaven until the time comes for
> God to restore everything, as he promised long ago through
> his holy prophets (Acts 3:19-21).

The renewal of all things, the reconciliation of all things, and the restoration of all things. That is how the Bible describes the end of the story.
It certainly includes the forgiveness purchased by Jesus for me and you,
but it is also a lot bigger than that.

Remember, we were created for Eden. The Bible is the story of God's
pursuit of human beings, not our pursuit of Him. The Bible begins with
God walking and speaking intimately with Adam and Eve. Once that
relationship is fractured through their rebellion, God immediately begins
the process of salvation and restoration. He calls a man, Abram, and
promises to make his descendants into a great nation through whom
will come One who will bless all the people of the earth.[3]

Hundreds of years later, God redeems His people, Israel, from slavery
in Egypt and dwells among them, guiding them with either a cloud
or a pillar of fire. He then instructs Moses to build the tabernacle, a
mobile sanctuary, so God can dwell among His people. His glory
(symbolic of His presence) descends on the tabernacle, and God lives
with His people, guiding, leading, and protecting them.

When the Israelites finally reach the land of Canaan and are
established in the promised land, God instructs Solomon to build a permanent temple so He can continue to dwell among His people. Again

His glory descends, and for centuries the people of Israel live with the assurance (and the fear) that their God lives among them.

At each step, God desired to come closer and closer to humanity. This journey reaches a climax in the coming of the Messiah, Jesus, who was God in human flesh. God dwelt among His people, not in a building they made, but as one of their own. He lived a fully human existence and suffered the worst this fallen world had to offer.

But even that was not close enough. The most astounding thing Jesus said to His disciples on the eve of His betrayal and crucifixion was that His leaving them and returning to the Father was for their good. What could possibly be good about Jesus leaving? His answer was that the Holy Spirit would come. The Spirit of Jesus would now dwell *in* His people and not just among them.

With each unfolding stage of His plan, God draws closer to His people. And the story of God's pursuit of us culminates in the restoration, renewal, and reconciliation of all things. The prophets had a specific way of talking about this restoration and reconciliation. This is how Isaiah described that coming day:

> Behold, I will create new heavens and a new earth. The former things will not be remembered, nor will they come to mind. But be glad and rejoice forever in what I will create, for I will create Jerusalem to be a delight and its people a joy. I will rejoice over Jerusalem and take delight in my people; the sound of weeping and of crying will be heard in it no more. Never again will there be in it an infant who lives but a few days, or an old man who does not live out his years; he who dies at a hundred will be thought a mere youth; he who fails to reach a hundred will be considered accursed. They will build houses and dwell in them; they will plant vineyards and eat their fruit. No longer will they build houses and others live in them, or plant and others eat. For as the days of a tree, so will be the days of my people; my chosen ones will long enjoy the works of their hands. They will not toil in vain or

> bear children doomed to misfortune; for they will be a people
> blessed by the LORD, they and their descendants with them
> (Isaiah 65:17-23).

Notice what is packed into this picture. Jerusalem is to be delight (we
saw that the word *Eden* meant "delight"). The new heavens and new
earth speak of restoration and renewal. Note that we will build houses
and plant vineyards; this is reminiscent of God's mandate to Adam
and Eve in Genesis 1–2 to work the earth. And see that the curses of
Genesis 3 are reversed. We will create, direct, arrange, and enjoy the
work of our hands. We will work, but evidently our work will no longer
feel like painful toil. We will do the things we love forever. We were
created for Eden, and God is at work to bring us back there.

If heaven for you is a fuzzy place in the clouds where we are bored
forever, think again. Heaven will be more alive, more dazzling, and
more compelling than the best we can imagine.

The story finishes (or begins, depending on how you want to look at it)
in Revelation 21–22. Here we get a picture of the end of this present
age, when all is made right and evil is forever banished from the universe. Notice what happens:

> Then I saw a new heaven and a new earth, for the first heaven
> and the first earth had passed away, and there was no longer
> any sea. I saw the Holy City, the new Jerusalem, coming
> down out of heaven from God, prepared as a bride beautifully
> dressed for her husband. And I heard a loud voice from the
> throne saying, "Now the dwelling of God is with men, and he
> will live with them. They will be his people, and God himself
> will be with them and be their God" (Revelation 21:1-3).

This is amazing, and it has been God's plan all along.[4] Our story ends
with heaven invading earth. God's realm comes to earth, and we all
dwell with Him on earth in resurrected bodies. The word *new* here
describing the new heaven and new earth doesn't mean that they are
not old, but rather that they are superior and improved in quality. In this
sense, *new* implies continuity with our present earth and heavens.[5]

Michael Wittmer puts it this way: "The Christian hope is not that someday we and our loved ones die and go to be with Jesus. Instead, the Christian hope is that our departure from this world is just the first leg of a journey that is round-trip."[6] This means that the earth will be our home.[7] We will continue to have a physical existence in glorified bodies.[8] We are not just passing through this world on the way to heaven. We are aliens and strangers toward the corrupt moral order of the earth, but Hegeman suggests the term "alienated residents" (as a better option than resident aliens) to describe our current physical existence.[9]

What We'll Do Forever

The next step is for us to see what we will do on this new earth:

> Then the angel showed me the river of the water of life, as clear as crystal, flowing from the throne of God and of the Lamb down the middle of the great street of the city. On each side of the river stood the tree of life, bearing twelve crops of fruit, yielding its fruit every month. And the leaves of the tree are for the healing of the nations. No longer will there be any curse. The throne of God and of the Lamb will be in the city, and his servants will serve him. They will see his face, and his name will be on their foreheads. There will be no more night. They will not need the light of a lamp or the light of the sun, for the Lord God will give them light. And they will reign for ever and ever (Revelation 22:1-5).

The restoration, renewal, and reconciliation of all things means a return to what God originally intended—our partnership with Him in Eden.

All of Scripture moves toward God taking up residence in our midst.[10] The end is the beginning of God's living with people on planet earth. In Genesis, we see a tree of life, rivers, and people living in significant relationship with God and each other, doing significant work with God. Now look at Revelation 22. Instead of a garden, we'll live in a city. The tree of the knowledge of good and evil is gone because evil was destroyed. But notice the parallels between Revelation 22 and Genesis 1–2: the river, the tree of life, the plants yielding fruit, and even the mention of curses, which are now reversed. God not only forgives us but also is working to bring everything back into His original design.

What does all of this have to do with our mortgage broker? He is preparing for heaven by doing his job today faithfully and with integrity. He will work in heaven just as he works now and just as Adam worked the garden. This is what it means to be masculine—to partner with God in ordering and stewarding creation. N.T. Wright puts it this way:

> The point of following Jesus isn't simply so that we can be sure of going to a better place than this after we die. Our future beyond death is enormously important, but the nature of the Christian hope is such that it plays back into the present life. We're called, here and now, to be instruments of God's new creation, the world-put-to-rights which has already been launched in Jesus and of which Jesus' followers are supposed to be not simply beneficiaries but also agents.[11]

Notice what we'll do on this renewed earth. We'll reign with God.[12] To reign means to actively participate with. This is a direct allusion to the work that was begun in the beginning of Genesis. I return to my partnership with God in the caretaking and stewarding of creation. But I can taste that now. I can prepare myself for what I'll be entrusted with in heaven. What we do here matters.

You and I were born to rule—to wield power, authority, and blessing in God's name. That is how our story begins (in Genesis), and that is how our story ends (in Revelation). Most of us feel as if heaven doesn't really have anything to do with how we live now. But that is not at all what the Scriptures say. What I do now matters forever. I don't arrive in heaven with just a ticket and without any consequences for the life I lived while on the earth.

> Do not be afraid, little flock, for your Father has been pleased to give you the kingdom. Sell your possessions and give to the

poor. Provide purses for yourselves that will not wear out, a treasure in heaven that will not be exhausted, where no thief comes near and no moth destroys (Luke 12:32-33).

"Well done, my good servant!" his master replied. "Because you have been trustworthy in a very small matter, take charge of ten cities" (Luke 19:17).

Who then is the faithful and wise servant, whom the master has put in charge of the servants in his household to give them their food at the proper time? It will be good for that servant whose master finds him doing so when he returns. I tell you the truth, he will put him in charge of all his possessions (Matthew 24:45-47).

His master replied, "Well done, good and faithful servant! You have been faithful with a few things; I will put you in charge of many things. Come and share your master's happiness" (Matthew 25:21).

Then the King will say to those on his right, "Come, you who are blessed by my Father; take your inheritance, the kingdom prepared for you since the creation of the world. For I was hungry and you gave me something to eat, I was thirsty and you gave me something to drink, I was a stranger and you invited me in, I needed clothes and you clothed me, I was sick and you looked after me, I was in prison and you came to visit me." Then the righteous will answer him, "Lord, when did we see you hungry and feed you, or thirsty and give you something to drink? When did we see you a stranger and invite you in, or needing clothes and clothe you? When did we see you sick or in prison and go to visit you?" The King will reply, "I tell you the truth, whatever you did for one of the least of these brothers of mine, you did for me" (Matthew 25:34-40).

By the grace God has given me, I laid a foundation as an expert builder, and someone else is building on it. But each one should be careful how he builds. For no one can lay any foundation other than the one already laid, which is Jesus Christ. If any man builds on this foundation using gold, silver, costly stones, wood, hay or straw, his work will be shown for what it is, because the Day will bring it to light. It will be revealed with fire, and the fire will test the quality of each man's work (1 Corinthians 3:10-13).

I tell you, use worldly wealth to gain friends for yourselves, so that when it is gone, you will be welcomed into eternal dwellings. Whoever can be trusted with very little can also be trusted with much, and whoever is dishonest with very little will also be dishonest with much. So if you have not been trustworthy in handling worldly wealth, who will trust you with true riches? And if you have not been trustworthy with someone else's property, who will give you property of your own (Luke 16:9-12)?

The very simple and yet overlooked point of these passages (and many others) is that our work here on earth matters. To some degree, our faithfulness with what we have been given here and now determines our usefulness in God's future kingdom. The reason my friend's work matters is that it is, in the words of Dallas Willard, "training for reigning." His faithfulness in little things today leads to God's entrusting him with larger things tomorrow.

The work we are called to do (Matthew 5:16; 1 Corinthians 15:58; Ephesians 2:10; Colossians 1:9-10; 2 Timothy 3:16-17; Hebrews 13:20-21) does not refer only to our religious deeds. The word *work* (or *deed* or *deeds*) in these passages is related to the Hebrew word used for *work* way back in Genesis 1–2. Our labor at our job, as a parent, or as a husband is all part of our cultural mandate today as well as part of what God has planned for us forever. Some of our work will actually follow us into heaven.[13]

Instead of seeing our jobs and lives on earth as simply biding time until we die or Jesus returns, we must see them in light of our original design and eternal destiny. This life is practice. We were created to rule, and we'll rule with God forever. The question is, will we be faithful with what we have been given in the meantime?

Heaven isn't filled with equally sized mansions. We are rewarded for the quality of labor we do while on the earth. What we do here matters. Relationships, money, gifts, talents, possessions—all of it is at our disposal, not for us to own, but for us to temporarily steward. This is how we see our work as redeemed: by realizing that what we do now is preparing us for life in the fullness of Jesus' kingdom.

So I think Paul would say this to our friend the mortgage broker:

> Slaves [for our purposes, we could substitute *employees*], obey your earthly masters in everything; and do it, not only when their eye is on you and to win their favor, but with sincerity of heart and reverence for the Lord. Whatever you do, work at it with all your heart, as working for the Lord, not for men, since you know that you will receive an inheritance from the Lord as a reward. It is the Lord Christ you are serving (Colossians 3:22-24).

What we are doing matters less than why we are doing it. A biblical masculine spirituality doesn't bother to discriminate between important and unimportant jobs or spiritual and sacred ones, but instead encourages men to do the best they can, for the glory of God, with whatever assignments fall their way. To use our everyday work to cooperate with God's invasion of the earth is the essence of following Jesus.

Part Three

IN THE BEDROOM

Chapter 6

NAKED AND UNASHAMED

Sex is like religion not only because it is objectively holy in itself but also because it gives us subjectively a foretaste of heaven, of the self-forgetting, self-transcending self-giving that is what our deepest hearts are designed for, long for and will not be satisfied until they have, because we are made in God's own image and this self-giving constitutes the inner life of the Trinity.

PETER KREEFT

As we noted in chapter 1, far too many of us begin the study of masculinity in Genesis 3 with the account of the fall of Adam and Eve and the entrance of sin and death into the world. Genesis 3 does show us the world as we now live in it, but Genesis 1–2 shows us the world as God intended. This is a significant oversight. Our story does not begin with sin, shame, and guilt. It begins much earlier than that. We neglect the true beginning of the story. In Genesis 1–2 we see a creation that is separate from God but that delights Him and reflects Him nevertheless.

The implications of this error are far-reaching. There is a temptation in Christian circles to be suspicious of creation. We are tempted to differentiate the spiritual from the material, the unseen world from what is seen. There are subtle implications that being made of flesh, with all of the attendant cravings, desires, and frailties, is inherently a bad thing or at least something less than what God had wanted for us.

We must constantly remind ourselves that being human and being male are good things. We are part of God's good creation. Using the bathroom, eating dinner, having sex—these things are not results of sin, they are results of God's good design for us. This is an important point. We far too often mistake the spiritual as being superior to the physical. The Bible makes no such judgment. Genesis 1–2 declares why.

These two paths—the path that begins with creation and the path that begins with the fall—often grow further apart when we come to the study of masculinity and femininity. For instance, many tremendously influential Christian books on masculinity locate the essence of masculinity in the aftermath of Genesis 3. Many authors suggest that the core of masculinity is located in conflict, antagonism, separation, and woundedness. This often describes what is, but it does not call us to what could be (what God intended for us). This theology isn't incorrect, but this concept of masculinity is simply incomplete. It cannot handle the sweeping diversity of masculine pictures and exhortations from the Scriptures.

Any theology of masculinity (or of humanity, for that matter) must begin with the creation poem of Genesis 1 and its companion narrative in Genesis 2. To do otherwise is to render us unable to make complete sense of the New Testament teachings regarding the relationships between men and women and especially between husbands and wives.

Flesh and Spirit

Most fundamentally, we have seen in the opening of Genesis that to be human and male is good. I don't mean good in the moral sense (under sin, none of us are good that way); rather, being human and masculine are good things. God seems to have intended that we always will be a union of the physical and the spiritual. Angels and demons and God

Himself are spiritual beings who can manifest themselves physically. Animals and plants (depending on how one defines souls or spirits) are primarily physical. Only in humanity did God join the spiritual and material realms together. David put it this way in Psalm 8:

> When I consider your heavens, the work of your fingers, the moon and the stars, which you have set in place, what is man that you are mindful of him, the son of man that you care for him? You made him a little lower than the heavenly beings and crowned him with glory and honor. You made him ruler over the works of your hands; you put everything under his feet: all flocks and herds, and the beasts of the field, the birds of the air, and the fish of the sea, all that swim the paths of the seas (Psalm 8:3-8).

We have a unique role in all creation to appreciate and enjoy God and all that He has made and to worship Him freely in response. To be human and male is good.

When Jesus appeared in human flesh, He underscored this point. God honored humanity by taking it upon Himself in the person of Jesus, who ate, slept, drank, worked, and played like all the rest of us. This point should dismiss any thought that human bodies are bad things. Jesus' resurrection was not an escape from the physical realm but a fulfillment of God's design. Paul explains in 1 Corinthians that we too will receive resurrection bodies. We not only are housed in physical bodies now but also will be housed in physical (though immortal and imperishable) bodies with God forever.

So to be made up of physical stuff—to have hunger and thirst and desire—is not a bad thing. We often mistake being human for being sinful.

Once we accept the goodness of our creation, we are ready to affirm our spiritual nature as well. Genesis 2:7 says that "the LORD God formed the man from the dust of the ground and breathed into his nostrils the breath of life, and the man became a living being." Some other translations write that God took Adam and "breathed his spirit" into him. In Hebrew, this is a fascinating wordplay. *Breath* and *spirit* share a common root, but the point for our purposes is that God made us to be not only physical but spiritual as well. This is something we share in common with God, one of the ways we reflect His image. We are more than just random atoms or material brains. Something immaterial about us is fundamentally who we are.

We know this. But beyond knowing it, we must consider its implications. We are spiritual beings, so we engage in spiritual activities. The corollary is this: Human activities are spiritual activities. Eating, drinking, mowing the yard, watching a movie—all of this is spiritual because it involves human beings who are spiritual.

So the things of the spirit are no better (and are sometimes more troublesome) than the things of the body. To be made of flesh and blood is good because God said so. Being a pastor is not more Christian than being a mortgage broker, nor is praying more Christian than eating. Paul says that whatever you do, even eating and drinking, you should do to the glory of God.[1] I don't know if Paul could have picked two more mundane human activities than eating and drinking. If our eating and drinking can glorify God, so can almost all human endeavors.

The cultural mandate we examined in chapter 3—to fill the earth, subdue it, rule over the animals, and tend the garden—affirms the value of ordinary human and masculine life.

> This is the positive reason for the sixteenth-century Protestant affirmation of ordinary life and culture, that is, of the normal practices of human hands and minds...We needn't become priests or nuns in order to have a vocation, and we needn't withdraw to monasteries to serve God maximally...work and play, friendship and marriage, business and art (probably even government) are all intrinsically good things and may all have a part in a Christian's vocation. God has "hallowed" these good things and called us to relish and employ them. A slice of bread or a game of soccer may tell us of God's goodness as surely, even if not as directly, as a tract, and this is true

even if the baker and the player do not realize their activity has been sponsored by God. The Christian at her drafting board may be engaged in "full-time Christian service," just as surely as the priest at his altar.[2]

It Is Good

All of this has phenomenal implications for men in their sexual relationships with women. Genesis 1 ends with the most incredible affirmation: Adam and Eve were naked, and they felt no shame.

Let that sink in a moment.

Think about the implications. Being naked was all that Adam and Eve knew. And their nakedness described their level of intimacy. No shame, no guilt, no barriers, no insecurity, no comparison or competition. Nothing but joy. Delight. Intimacy.

This is a big deal. Here is why this is so important: *We were sexual before we were sinful.* In other words, the sexual part of us—the part that experiences arousal, passion, release—was all part of God's good creation. That means that although our sin has tainted our sexuality, being sexual is still a good thing.

Much of the church of Jesus has missed this. As a result, people get the impression that sex shouldn't be discussed within the community of followers of Jesus except to remind us to stay away from it. But the Scriptures don't start there. In Genesis 1–2, being sexual is part of being human. And being human is good. Therefore, being sexual is good too. Far too many of us look at our sexuality as a curse instead of as the good gift of a gracious God.

Think about it. God is the author of sex. This isn't the enemy's territory; this is something that God ordained to be enjoyed and to knit the hearts and bodies of two people together. This may seem obvious to some of us, but to many others, this is revolutionary and liberating. All that I remember hearing from my church about sex came from an older guy in our youth group who sat down with me to talk about "the biological hand-grenade ladder." The idea was that there were levels of sexual intimacy, and the further one went up the ladder (which ranged from kissing to French kissing, petting, heavy petting, and intercourse), the more one would experience the explosive results of sexual sin. Instead of helping me resist temptation, it just made temptation even more tempting. If something was that big a deal, I wanted to find out why.

That was all I heard from my church. Stay away. Don't indulge. Don't talk about it. And the implication was loud and clear: Being sexual was being bad. Instead of giving people a beautiful and compelling picture of sex that awakens in us a hunger to hold out for what God intended for us, my church instead told me to refrain from my God-given desires for no other reason than because they said so.

The result? Telling a 13-year-old boy about heavy petting (the term conjured forbidden love in a zoo) did nothing but increase my interest in the subject. Once I experienced heavy petting, I discovered what all the fuss was about but wasn't equipped to understand why I shouldn't have such fun. This was my first encounter with sexuality, but my church didn't have much to say about it.

Instead of beginning with sexuality's rightful place among the best gifts God gives the human beings He loves and created, the church begins in Genesis 3 with the fall of sexuality. That is part of our story, but it is not the whole thing. The Bible begins instead with a resounding affirmation: They were naked and unashamed. They were to fill the earth and multiply. How were they going to do this? By having lots of sex and making lots of babies! Of course, God could have had human beings procreate through planting seeds in the ground, but He chose to make the process much more fun!

We find this affirmation of sex and sexuality throughout the Scriptures. In the Old Testament, God uses marital, romantic language to describe His passion for His people. He expresses jealousy at Israel's unfaithfulness and uses the prophet Hosea as a picture of how faithful He is to faithless Israel.

One of the clearest expressions of God's blessing of sexuality is in the Old Testament poem Song of Songs. There are many different ways of approaching this book. Some understand it to be a metaphor expressing God's love for His people. Others see it as a romantic, passionate, and erotic story of love between a man and a woman. My view is that we should understand it as both. The Bible often uses the intimate relationship between man and woman to express God's love for His people.[3] I think it is appropriate to see Song of Songs as such a love story that points to much larger spiritual realities.

God's affirmation of sexuality is found all over the poem:

> Let him kiss me with the kisses of his mouth—for your love is more delightful than wine (1:2).

> My lover is mine and I am his; he browses among the lilies. Until the day breaks and the shadows flee, turn, my lover, and be like a gazelle or like a young stag on the rugged hills (2:16-17).

> Awake, north wind, and come, south wind! Blow on my garden, that its fragrance may spread abroad. Let my lover come into his garden and taste its choice fruits (4:16).

> How beautiful you are and how pleasing, O love, with your delights. Your stature is like that of the palm, and your breasts like clusters of fruit. I said, "I will climb the palm tree; I will take hold of its fruit" (7:6-8).

> Come, my lover, let us go to the countryside, let us spend the night in the villages. Let us go early to the vineyards to see if the vines have budded, if their blossoms have opened, and if the pomegranates are in bloom—there I will give you my love. The mandrakes send out their fragrance, and at our door is every delicacy, both new and old, that I have stored up for you, my lover (7:11-13). [Both mandrakes and pomegranates were considered aphrodisiacs.]

And I'm skipping some of the more erotic stuff. In fact, some commentators argue that God only has one sentence in the whole book. Right after the couple is married and has sex, God says "Eat, O friends and drink; drink your fill, O lovers."[4]

The point again is this: Being sexual is a good thing. The man and woman enjoyed wholeness and eroticism before the fall; the fall just perverted and tainted it.

Often the message we hear from the church community is the opposite: Sex is unspiritual and so are our bodies. This leaves us confused about the role our bodies play in our spiritual lives. We think our bodies don't matter, that Jesus just cares about our hearts or souls and our bodies get left behind. But Jesus inhabited a body and saved us with His body, and He was (and we will be) resurrected in a new body. Bodies are good things, as are their desires.

We have often been taught, either directly or through implication or omission, only that our bodies and their desires are corrupted. Because of this, many Christian couples who have abstained from sex before marriage struggle with feeling guilty about sex after their vows. People discover they can't flip a switch and feel good about their sexuality if all they have been told is that it is off-limits and to be avoided at all costs. In stark contrast, the Scriptures declare that sexuality is a great gift from God.

Spotting the Counterfeits

Underlying this playful point is a serious one. Being sexual is a necessary part of being male. It isn't a bad thing to want sex, enjoy sex, and wish we had more sex. We must continually place our sexuality (and everything else about us) under the kingship of Jesus, but doing so does not take the fun out of it.

The church has done a great disservice to us by remaining silent on this issue or telling us to stay away from sex. God's intent is that we, as fundamentally spiritual human beings, would discuss all of what it means to follow Him in the course of real life. In Deuteronomy, God commanded His people to talk about His instructions during the mundane activities of life:

> These commandments that I give you today are to be upon your hearts. Impress them on your children. Talk about them when you sit at home and when you walk along the road, when you lie down and when you get up. Tie them as symbols on your hands and bind them on your foreheads. Write them on the doorframes of your houses and on your gates (Deuteronomy 6:6-9).

God's commands had everything to do with how the Israelites lived their daily lives. No subjects were off-limits. God's people understood that everything about their lives mattered to Him and that as a community they were to discuss everything about life together. I don't know when or where or why God's people ceased talking about sex, but these days, churches rarely discuss it in a healthy way. I love how Tommy Nelson has said it: "We should not be ashamed to discuss what God was not ashamed to create."[5]

We will learn about sex. In the locker room, online, from friends or music, or at the magazine rack, we will learn. And so will our kids. The question is not whether they will learn but rather how they will do so and whose opinion they will trust.

The church needs to remind men that we were created to be naked and unashamed. We must be recaptured by the beauty, holiness, and majesty of what God intended for human sexuality. Saying no to sex outside of marriage seems cruel and arbitrary apart from saying yes to sex within marriage. Would we rather have $5 today or $5 million in three years? That is what is at issue. God is no killjoy. As we'll see in the next chapter, the only real sex that takes place is within marriage. Sex outside that context isn't really sex at all.[6] The problem is that we love the counterfeits because we don't have to deal with the problems of the real thing.

I know a secret service agent who investigates monetary counterfeit schemes. He pointed out to me that such agents are trained not by studying the counterfeits but by immersing themselves in the real thing. They don't study all the ways that money can be faked; they only examine the real thing. That is why they can spot the counterfeits—they have been trained to recognize the genuine item.

The same is true for us. We need to be immersed in the goodness of sexuality so we can recognize (and reject) the impostors that come our way, not out of guilt and duty, but in joy and anticipation.

Understanding the goodness of sex and God's affirmation of it frees us from much that is false regarding sexuality in the church and culture. Jesus, for instance, was fully human, so He was sexual. The Bible also comments that He was tempted in every way, yet was without sin.[7] So we can safely assume Jesus experienced sexual temptation yet didn't sin. Temptation itself, therefore, isn't sin. We can be tempted all the time, but that by itself is only an affirmation of God's good gift of sexuality. To be tempted doesn't mean we have crossed the line.

This was liberating for me to learn because I was raised to think that sexual feelings *themselves* were bad. To have sexual desire toward anyone was shameful. But the Scriptures don't teach that at all. In fact, God never condemns normal healthy sexual desire. He does condemn lust, which is the corruption of healthy desire. (I think it was Martin Luther who, when commenting on this issue, said, "A bird may get stuck in your hair, but it doesn't have to build a nest.") In other words, normal sexual desire becomes lustful when it is intentionally cultivated and fed images that would be wrong if they were to play out in real life. I think most of us know the difference. I experienced freedom when I understood that simply finding a woman sexually appealing isn't itself a sinful act.

An appreciation for the goodness of sexuality also frees us in marriage. I have seen far too many couples wrecked early in marriage because of this issue. They have abstained from sex outside of marriage but for the wrong reasons. Maybe they grew up thinking sex was bad. Or maybe they were trying to impress God or their youth pastor or something. But they arrived on their honeymoon night only to find that the switch that was supposed to be flipped during the wedding ceremony making sex okay was somehow stuck, and they have nagging feelings of guilt and shame. I have talked with several men who couldn't wait to have sex with their brides but then turned away from sex, feeling ashamed because it still seemed wrong.

This is where Genesis 1 comes in and why it is so important. Every other conversation we have about sexuality has to begin here or else we either turn against God (He is a killjoy; He is not good for giving us these desires and calling us to wait) or ourselves (these feelings are wrong; I am bad for having these feelings). Both paths lead to great harm and frustration.

We don't abstain from sex outside of marriage because we are good little Christian boys or because sexuality is a bad thing. We hold out for the best sex possible, sex without guilt, shame, disease, comparison, and insecurity. Sex that takes us beyond our genitals and ourselves. I think the most erotic picture of sexuality is of two clueless virgins on their honeymoon night, discovering this great gift and realizing they have a lifetime together to figure it all out.

Ultimately, sex and our desire for it points to God. Guys need God because guys love sex. Something about our sexuality is transcendent and mysterious. There is something of great power, something beyond the simple ability to procreate. We are spiritual and physical beings, and sex unites these two parts of us in ways that can either bring glory and honor to God as its author or cause much damage.

We long for the return to Eden, to be naked and unashamed once more.

> Sexuality is a beautiful, good, extremely powerful, sacred energy given us by God and experienced in every cell of our being as an irrepressible urge to overcome our incomplete-ness, to move toward unity and consummation with that which is beyond us. It is also the pulse to celebrate, to give and to

receive delight, to find our way back to the Garden of Eden where we can be naked, shameless, and without worry and work as we make love in the moonlight.[8]

Men crave intimacy in ways we don't even understand, and we really don't know how to find it. Most of us no longer see our bodies as sacred even though Paul talks about them as being "temples of the Holy Spirit."[9] In the Old Testament, God cared about the exact dimensions and smallest details of both the tabernacle and temple because He would dwell there.[10] We must reclaim the sacred nature of both sex and the human body and view them as sacred the same way that God cared about the temple.

The affirmation that sex is good and is of God must frame any other discussion of the subject. We can still be naked and unashamed. Under Jesus, reclaiming what is rightfully His, we are able to embrace the good gifts of sex and sexual desire. There is hope. Our struggles, our failures, and our mistakes in this area no longer have to define us. And for those who wait (and wonder if they are waiting in vain), the wait is worth it. Not because you will always have shaking-the-walls sex but because sex is good and God delights when we enjoy it without guilt, shame, or comparison.

Chapter 7

NOT ALL ELECTRIC SHOCKS ARE BAD

It should be obvious why the church so often falls on the side of repression, rather than celebration, of sexuality: No human longing is more powerful, and more difficult to rein in. Sex has enough combustive force to incinerate conscience, vows, family commitments, religious devotion, or anything else in its path.

PHILIP YANCEY

In the last chapter, we saw that human bodies are good and that they were made for sex. Sexuality isn't a curse; it is God's good gift to men and expresses the reality that we are both physical as well as spiritual beings. The early chapters of Genesis not only encourage us that sexuality is good but also caution us that it is powerful:

For this reason a man will leave his father and mother and be united to his wife, and they will become one flesh (Genesis 2:24).

Nothing else that can happen between two human beings has this effect. In no other way can two people join themselves together to be one. God's gift of sex is good, but it is also powerful. It can be a source of great joy, filled with meaning, or it can cause great shame and harm. The only thing strong enough to handle its power is marriage: one man and one woman in permanent, monogamous, covenantal relationship.[1]

The implication is that sex is good, but it can be used in ways that cause deep and lasting damage. The result of the sex act is that two people become one flesh. (Interestingly, the term *one* here is the same used in Deuteronomy to describe how God the Trinity is one.) In the act of sex, two individuals become bonded together in such a way as to create one person. This is no mere joining of bodies, but something deep and mystical. This oneness serves as the basis for the sexual ethic of the New Testament—that two people have joined themselves together in a way that should not be undone.[2] Ronald Rolheiser highlights the significance of sex:

> Sex is not just like anything else, despite our culture's protest. Its fire is so powerful, so precious, so close to the heart and soul of a person, and so godly, that it either gives life or it takes it away. It can never be casual, but is either a sacrament or a destructive act.[3]

This is the reason the Scriptures warn against the inappropriate use of sexuality. We can cause (and suffer) great harm when we abuse our sexuality. We know this. We see the carnage of this everywhere today. But that doesn't stop us from finding out for ourselves.

Here we see the double standard of our sinful masculine hearts. We don't call the electrician unfair or a killjoy because he warns us against the dangers of electricity. We don't label judges who harshly sentence drunk drivers as no fun or rigid because drunks behind the wheel can do a great deal of harm with a car. Anything that is powerful has rules that govern its use. Electricity, cars, nuclear power...all are powerful and come with rules that ensure the power is harnessed to achieve its intended end. The same is true with sexuality. But instead of recognizing that God, like the electrician or judge, issues rules for our own good, we seem to think God gave us these desires and then arbitrarily commanded us to say no to them because He enjoys watching our misery.

The truly Christian view of sex is not negative: "We can't have sex outside of marriage." Instead, it is a positive declaration of God's gift: "Sex was made for marriage, and marriage was made for sex." The kind of union described in Genesis 2 is the only thing strong enough to handle the power of human sexuality. Without the bigger picture in view, the commands to say no make little sense. We must look at the entire story of sexuality and not just pick and choose a few proof texts that say no.

Sex involves the whole person. The problem with strip clubs and porn isn't that they are too sexual; the problem with them is that they are not sexual enough. They totally eliminate relationship and restrict sexuality to the genitals and the act itself. The biblical view is much richer and fuller.[4] It is far more than what you do with your genitals; it has to do with beauty, passion, romance, walking on the beach, holding hands, kissing, laughing together. This is the stuff of sexuality. It is so much bigger than what the world presents to us.

A strong faith and a strong sex drive are not mutually exclusive. God's commands are for our good, and sexuality is an expression of His goodness. We must come to understand and believe this. The commands restricting sexual intercourse to marriage are not given because God is a killjoy.

I think we all know this deep down. People experience shame after a one-night stand with someone they just met, and that shame is totally absent from what happens when a husband and wife make love. We may not like it, or we may choose to ignore it, but I suspect our souls are hardwired to know the difference between what God intended and what we often settle for.

Many of us decide to live according to our own sexual boundaries. We will learn about sexuality, and we will be sexual. This is the way God made us. Unfortunately, few people in the church are bold enough to show us how our faith and sexuality fit together, and few are honest enough to show us how to handle sexual sin when we fail. The fruit of the church's silence about sexuality stands out in the lives of its people. The amount of adultery, premarital sex, inappropriate divorce, sexual experimentation, lust, and masturbation is staggering.[5]

We should also understand that living outside of God's instructions about sex says something about what we believe about God. If God is really good, His commands for us are good. By living in rebellion against His commands, we are saying that we know what is good for us better than He does. We are saying (with the way we are living) that His boundaries are not as good as ours; we know better. And if we believe His commands are not good, we believe He is not good either.

If we are living in sexual sin, we are declaring that God is not good.

Our problem is that we would rather indulge in the counterfeits of intimacy than face the issues of the real thing. Porn or a willing hookup can give us the satisfaction we want without demanding relationship, commitment, or integrity. So we settle for less than what God intended and then blame Him for setting up the boundaries that provide the kind of sex we're missing and can't find apart from Him.

That is what is at issue here. God is no killjoy; instead, He warns us about the power of sexuality and has created marriage to be the place where it can be properly expressed.[6]

Sex and Marriage

The Bible begins with a marriage in Genesis 2:24. It also ends with a marriage.

> Let us rejoice and be glad and give him glory! For the wedding of the Lamb has come, and his bride has made herself ready. Fine linen, bright and clean, was given her to wear... Blessed are those who are invited to the wedding supper of the Lamb!...I saw the Holy City, the new Jerusalem, coming down out of heaven from God, prepared as a bride beautifully dressed for her husband (Revelation 19:7-9; 21:2).

Marriage is the analogy the Bible uses most often to describe the love and passion God has for His people. God portrays Himself as a faithful husband throughout the Old Testament. When Israel was faithful to Him, she was described as a bride; when Israel worshipped other gods, she was described as an adulterer. A few examples will make this point:

> As a young man marries a maiden, so will your sons marry you; as a bridegroom rejoices over his bride, so will your God rejoice over you (Isaiah 62:5).

> "In that day," declares the LORD, "you will call me 'my husband'; you will no longer call me 'my master.' I will remove the names of the Baals from her lips; no longer will their names be invoked...I will betroth you to me forever; I will betroth you in righteousness and justice, in love and compassion. I will betroth you in faithfulness, and you will acknowledge the LORD" (Hosea 2:16-17,19-20).

> I gave faithless Israel her certificate of divorce and sent her away because of all her adulteries (Jeremiah 3:8).

I have heard people speculate that God created us with sexual passion so He would have language intense enough to describe how He loves His people and desires relationship with them. That passion also gives us language to depict how God feels when we turn our allegiance and worship away from Him and give it to others.

Signs, Props, and Pointers

Scripture uses marriage and the sexual intimacy within it to point to something bigger. In the New Testament, it points to the relationship between Christ and the church.

> Husbands, love your wives, just as Christ loved the church and gave himself up for her to make her holy, cleansing her by the washing with water through the word, and to present her to himself as a radiant church, without stain or wrinkle or any

other blemish, but holy and blameless. In this same way, husbands ought to love their wives as their own bodies. He who loves his wife loves himself. After all, no one ever hated his own body, but he feeds it and cares for it, just as Christ does the church—for we are members of his body. For this reason a man will leave his father and mother and be united to his wife, and the two will become one flesh. This is a profound mystery—but I am talking about Christ and the church (Ephesians 5:25-32).

God knows we are forgetful people. That is why He always uses a prop or sign to remind His people of His faithfulness to His promises. He ties a physical object to a spiritual concept in order for His people to understand and remember the point. With Noah, God used a rainbow as the sign of His promise never again to flood the earth. With Abraham, it was circumcision. With Israel, it was the sacrificial system. And for those who follow Jesus Christ, it is baptism and communion.

A sign of a covenant is a means not only of remembering the reality but also of somehow partaking in it. The union of marriage is an emotional, physical, and spiritual covenant between two people and God. Sexual intercourse is the sign that allows a husband and wife to participate in the reality of the covenant itself. But it goes beyond the relationship between husband and wife. As Paul teaches, the covenant of marriage describes how God desires intimacy with us. That is why he hates divorce—it destroys the sign of His faithfulness to us. So sex is never just about sex, and marriage is never just about marriage.

Men were designed to be sexual beings and to express our sexuality in the ways we relate to others. God created sex, and He uses its power and intimacy as a way to describe His faithfulness and passion for His people. Then He calls them to express their sexual desire within the bounds of covenant relationship.

We must remind ourselves of these things because somehow, somewhere, the church has gotten off track and has taught that sexuality itself is sinful. Sexuality is a wonderful and awesome thing. It is woven into the very fabric of our humanness. It is time the church started to recognize that all that we say about sexual ethics to our world must begin with this resounding declaration: It is good!

Yet the very first pages of the Bible temper that declaration by warning of its power. In no other way are two people bonded into one flesh. Deeper than the mere joining of genitals, sex involves the whole person and is the truest joining of bodies, hearts, and souls. The prohibition of sexual activity outside heterosexual marriage is based on this profound insight: Intercourse creates this mysterious one-flesh union. Interestingly, the Hebrew word for intercourse means "to know." Sex gives us a special kind of knowledge; a new kind of intimacy comes into being, and this reality is called "one flesh." Sexuality comes from places deep within us and is the only way we can unite our lives with another. The sexual encounter does something that, for better or worse, cannot be undone. Sex outside of marriage violates the nature of the act itself; it is to engage in a life-uniting act without life-uniting commitment. This sin is not irreversible, but it requires the healing touch of God.

Once framed this way, the teachings on sexuality throughout the Bible make sense. All of the rules in Bible are intended to protect God's people and to point and return them to the created order, the world as God meant it to be. From Genesis to Revelation, through boundaries, rules, examples, and admonitions, God articulates His original intent for sex: that it be expressed in marriage. Song of Solomon is the perfect expression of what this sexuality, restored by law and grace, looks like.

Bringing Sacred Back

We can express God's intent for sexual intimacy most simply this way:

It is all sex.

It is all reserved for marriage.

Our culture conveniently distinguishes between different kinds of sex, oral sex being the most common variation. But this distinction is unknown in the Scriptures. There is simply no way that two people can be naked and intimate in these ways while keeping our technical definitions of virginity in place. The whole thing is sex, and the whole thing is reserved for marriage. I love how subtle and unclear the following passages are:

> But among you [God's people] there must not be even a hint of sexual immorality, or of any kind of impurity, or of greed, because these are improper for God's holy people (Ephesians 5:3).

> Marriage should be honored by all, and the marriage bed kept pure, for God will judge the adulterer and the sexually immoral (Hebrews 13:4).

> It is God's will that you should be sanctified: that you should avoid sexual immorality; that each of you should learn to control his body in a way that is holy and honorable, not in passionate lust like the heathen, who do not know God (1 Thessalonians 4:3-4).

> Do you not know that your bodies are members of Christ himself? Shall I then take the members of Christ and unite them with a prostitute? Never! Do you not know that he who unites himself with a prostitute is one with her in body? For it is said, "The two will become one flesh." But he who unites himself with the Lord is one with him in spirit. Flee sexual immorality. All other sins a man commits are outside his body, but he who sins sexually sins against his own body. Do you not know that your body is a temple of the Holy Spirit, who is in you, whom you have received from God? You are not your own; you were bought at a price. Therefore honor God with your body (1 Corinthians 6:15-20).

The primary concern in these passages is that believers avoid *pornia*—a Greek word that the New Testament uses 55 times and is translated as *sexual immorality, lust,* or *adultery.* It refers to illicit sexual activity and covers a broad range of sexual transgression.

We may not like it, but to deny the clarity of these passages along with their implications for how we live is to deny the authority of Scripture in our lives. No amount of biblical gymnastics can diminish the clarity and force of these commands.

But what about the so-called gray areas leading up to sexual intercourse? Many of us have wondered, *How far can we go?* Again, to the Hebrew mind, the whole experience—from holding hands to intercourse—is sex. All our distinctions and questions are really designed to justify our behavior. I think the clearest articulation of God's standard before marriage is the thrice-quoted line in Song of Solomon, "Do not arouse or awaken love until it so desires," or, as we may put it, do not arouse or awaken love until it can be fulfilled in a holy way.[8]

To be sure, this is a moving target. When we were dating, my wife and I were sometimes safe holding hands or kissing, but sometimes we couldn't be in the same room because she couldn't keep her hands off me. (Now that we are married, she can keep her hands off me just fine.) But the point is simple enough: Don't get the sexual engine started until you can allow it to take you to holy, married sex.

What about "look but don't touch"? Jesus dealt with the issue of lust (which is different from the normal sexual desire we looked at in the last chapter) in Matthew 5:28: "But I tell you that anyone who looks at a woman lustfully has already committed adultery with her in his heart." I think this verse also speaks to us about the issue of masturbation because most men cannot masturbate without lusting.

Scripture doesn't come out and say, "Don't masturbate." But it doesn't encourage it either. It is difficult to put in the right or wrong category. The Bible isn't shy about mentioning sex, but it doesn't mention masturbation. It doesn't seem to be the most important issue from God's perspective, but masturbation removes sexual pleasure from the intimacy of God-intended relationship and makes orgasm the most important thing. God has more for us than that.

I know how restrictive Matthew 5:28 sounds. Believe me, I know! I hit puberty at 12 and married at 29—I *know*. But somehow, through God's grace and some self-control, I managed to make it to my wedding night. To simply declare that it is all sex and all of it is reserved for marriage doesn't help us when we are single and dealing with loneliness, temptation, insecurity, or God-given desire. It doesn't help us when our marriages are unsatisfying or once-a-month sex isn't what we had waited for. I know. I fight the same battles too.

But if we are to be men who find wholeness, forgiveness, and joy in our sexuality, we must start by telling the truth. Sex is God's good gift to us. But it is also powerful. And because it is powerful, it must be respected and expressed wisely. None of this impugns God's goodness because we use powerful things carefully all the time. But sex is unique.

I want to remind us that the journey to being godly, male, and sexual all at the same time begins with God's intention for sex. Any man who violates God's laws only ends up proving them rather than destroying them. The words of God are undeniable and unalterable.

The Scriptures teach that sex outside of marriage is wrong even though it may feel great. We don't always subjectively feel the harm of sexual sin. Sex is where our emotions are the least reliable. The recognition that sex is life-uniting means that something profound is happening whether we feel it or not. Sex returns us to the oneness described and promised in Genesis; it is precisely because something real happens during sex that it is so controversial.

So where does that leave us? If we are to become truly sexually free and healthy men, we must leave behind our self-deceptions and self-rationalizations. As much as we may wish it otherwise, the Bible really is clear on this.

But this doesn't say a thing to a bachelor about how to navigate the temptations of dating and engagement without falling into sin. Nor does it help us when our sex lives as married men are less than we feel we were promised. Know this: Hope is out there. But there are no simple solutions or quick fixes. The promise and hope of the gospel of Jesus is that He forgives our sins and makes our souls pure and white as snow. This is where true masculine sexuality begins. But we must first recognize our need for help and forgiveness.

Chapter 8

VICTORIA'S OTHER SECRET

> There are two ways of being a prophet. One is to tell the enslaved that they can be free. It is the difficult path of Moses. The second is to tell those who think they are free that they are in fact enslaved. This is the even more difficult path of Jesus.
>
> RICHARD ROHR

God created sex, it is good, and it is powerful. These realities must frame our discussion of masculine sexuality. Sex is not dirty or bad, nor can we take it so casually that we can do anything we want with it.

Unfortunately, because of the sin in our hearts, the fallenness of the world, and the silence of the church, the shame and abuse of sexuality is so pervasive that purity and virtue are the exception in the church rather than the rule. This is the most common issue dealt with in pastoral counseling. The carnage in this area is vastly greater than the harm done in any other. Fortunately, the Scriptures give us insight into how we found ourselves in this condition so that we may find the way out.[1]

The Descent

The opening chapters of Genesis trace our descent into our current condition.[2] God gave Adam and Eve the entire garden and all that was in it to steward, work, and enjoy. He only commanded them not to eat of the tree of the knowledge of good and evil. That was the only rule. It was the only restriction on their unlimited joy, freedom, and delight.

A serpent appears (whom we know from other texts to be Satan, our adversary and accuser) and begins to sow seeds of doubt in our original parents' minds. The pattern is instructive; Satan has not had to deviate from it since. This pattern is what I call the "descent," and it is what leads to sexual sin and ultimately results from it. This is what no one told us in high school sex education.

1. Satan begins by cultivating ingratitude. He focuses Eve's attention on the one restriction in the entire garden.

> "Did God really say, 'You must not eat from any tree in the garden'?" The woman said to the serpent, "We may eat fruit from the trees in the garden, but God did say, 'You must not eat fruit from the tree that is in the middle of the garden, and you must not touch it, or you will die'" (Genesis 3:1-3).

Satan is highly intelligent. Eve and Adam lived in perfect *shalom* with God, each other, and creation. They could do anything and could have anything. No shame, no sin, no guilt. In a garden full of yes, Satan directed Eve's attention to the one no God had commanded. Never mind that God had said yes to the entire garden. Never mind that God might know what He was doing. The best work of the enemy was getting Eve and Adam to focus on the one thing they *couldn't* do.

Our enemy wishes the same for us. How many men spend their lives chasing after things they don't have rather than enjoying the things they do have?

2. This leads to idolatry—denying that God has our best interests in mind.

> "You will not surely die," the serpent said to the woman. "For God knows that when you eat of it your eyes will be opened, and you will be like God, knowing good and evil" (Genesis 3:4-5).

"Because God has given you a no," the serpent argues, "He must not be good. He must be holding out on you. He knows that you will be like Him." Satan tempts them to walk outside what God had commanded them to do. He invites them to doubt God's goodness and faithfulness in even giving them the command. He entices them to place themselves at the center of their world, to build their own kingdom instead of God's and to follow their own wills instead of His. This is the temptation of every one of us since then: Who will rule our lives? God or us? Who will call the shots, make the rules, and get the credit for how we live? Each of us makes this choice, and it is at the heart of original sin.

3. Immorality comes next.

> When the woman saw that the fruit of the tree was good for food and pleasing to the eye, and also desirable for gaining wisdom, she took some and ate it. She also gave some to her husband, who was with her, and he ate it (Genesis 3:6).

Notice the progression. Focus on the no and ignore all the yeses. Because there is a no at all, God must not be good, and therefore we are better at knowing what is best for us. So Adam and Eve step outside of God's will for them. This is what immorality is. Look at Satan's claim: "You will not surely die." He tempts them to deny the consequences of their disobedience. "It won't hurt," "it isn't hurting anyone else," or "everyone does it" are common variations on this theme.

4. Imprisonment is the result.

> So the LORD God banished him from the Garden of Eden to work the ground from which he had been taken. After he drove the man out, he placed on the east side of the Garden of Eden cherubim and a flaming sword flashing back and forth to guard the way to the tree of life (Genesis 3:23-24).

Notice the nature of God's judgment in this passage. God's judgment isn't so much allowing us to be enslaved to things that are bad (though that happens). Rather, His judgment is most clearly expressed when He banishes us from things that are good. Adam and Eve were banned from Eden, not locked into somewhere else. That is the nature of God's judgment: We miss the best He has for us.

To sum up, here is the descent in Genesis 3:

1. Ingratitude—we focus on the rules and not the blessings.

2. Idolatry—because God places rules and restrictions on our freedom, He must not have our best interests in mind. Because God says no, He must not be good. We convince ourselves we know better.

3. Immorality—we deny the consequences and step out in disobedience.

4. Imprisonment—we lose the good that we would have had otherwise.

The Falling

Genesis 3 records the fall. Romans 1 records the falling. Genesis 3 is about Adam and Eve in the past. Romans 1 is about you and me in the present. Genesis 3 is past tense. Romans 1 is present tense. Our adversary has never had to improve upon what worked in duping Adam and Eve; we see the same descent in us today.

When we look at all the carnage, loneliness, and alienation in relationships and sexuality in our culture—the movie stars with perfect bodies and fame and fortune but who can't seem to stay married, for example—we each somehow delude ourselves into thinking that it will be different with us. This is the lie we want to expose in this section.

> The wrath of God is being revealed from heaven against all the godlessness and wickedness of men who suppress the truth by their wickedness, since what may be known about God is plain to them, because God has made it plain to them. For since the creation of the world God's invisible

qualities—his eternal power and divine nature—have been clearly seen, being understood from what has been made, so that men are without excuse (Romans 1:18-20).

Paul begins this section of Romans 1 by reminding us that God's judgment isn't just in the future. What he is recording for us is reenacted presently—it is "being revealed." God's wrath is not just something in the past (where it was poured out on Jesus) or waiting in the future (when we get to heaven or hell). It is something that is being "revealed" now.

Notice also that Paul claims that nobody is born an atheist; we all have an instinctive and soulish awareness of something bigger than us. We simply have to look out our windows for clues as to who or what that is. Paul says that because we are born into rebellion against God, we suppress the truth of God within us in order to go our own way. Paul traces out the results. Note the presence of the same pattern of descent that we encountered in Genesis 3.

Ingratitude

> For although they knew God, they neither glorified him as God nor gave thanks to him, but their thinking became futile and their foolish hearts were darkened (Romans 1:21).

Notice that this is where sexual sin starts: with our view of God and His gifts. Paul won't mention sexual sin until verse 24. We are Adam and Eve all over again. Instead of focusing on the yes of God in our lives, we focus on the no—on what we cannot have. This is true of us almost everywhere. We are incredibly ungrateful people. God rebuked the nation of Israel over and over again in the Old Testament for their ingratitude as He continually reminded them of His faithfulness. And I wonder if He feels the same way about us.

Gratitude is a basic orientation toward life that recognizes that we are undeserving and weak people and that everything has been given to us as a gift. I am not entitled to anything, not even life, liberty, and the pursuit of happiness. We can't control our heartbeat, the way air and carbon dioxide are exchanged in our lungs, or even the way we digest food. Despite our protests to the contrary, we are not in control over much in our lives. We didn't pick our parents, our personalities, or our natural abilities or disabilities. We didn't choose where or when to be born, nor will most of us have much say in when we die. The Scriptures are clear about this:

> Now listen, you who say, "Today or tomorrow we will go to this or that city, spend a year there, carry on business and make money." Why, you do not even know what will happen tomorrow. What is your life? You are a mist that appears for a little while and then vanishes. Instead, you ought to say, "If it is the Lord's will, we will live and do this or that." As it is you boast and brag. All such boasting is evil (James 4:13-16).

> The God who made the world and everything in it is the Lord of heaven and earth and does not live in temples built by human hands. And he is not served by human hands, as if he needed anything, because he himself gives all men life and breath and everything else. From one man he made every nation of men that they should inhabit the whole earth; and he determined the set times for them and the exact places where they should live (Acts 17:24-26).

As participants in Western culture, you and I are encouraged to adopt a deep sense of entitlement. That is the heart of our consumer culture: You can have it your way; you deserve what you want. From clothes to cereal, radio and TV stations, and shampoo, we are overwhelmed with choices. We walk around each day asking one simple question: What do I want? We protect our right to choose, to speak, and to do with our bodies what we wish. All of this is fine, but it can't help but undermine our sense of gratitude to some degree.

The obsession with choice infects the church. If you don't like one, there are dozens of others down the street that might better cater to your preferences.

Most of us are hardly ever thankful about our sexuality. Singles want to be married, married people want to be single (at least some of the time), and married people with kids often want to enjoy the lifestyle they had when they were newly married. A man may have a great job, great friends and family, health, faith, and a career, but the enemy tries to get him to focus on the no. So that is all he thinks about. Instead of being thankful to God for the thousands of blessings poured out to us each day, we obsess over what is forbidden.

This doesn't change when we get married. The problem with every no is that it always leads to another one. As a married man, I can have sex—but only with the same person the rest of my life. Once the awe and wonder of sex fades, a new lie sets in: This will be boring. Is this the last set of breasts I am allowed to look at (guilt free) for the rest of my life? So the same trap works: Instead of delighting in the wife of my youth, cultivating thankfulness for the gift she is to me, I focus on the new no, and the process starts all over again.

Ingratitude allows us to rationalize all sorts of sexual compromises. What is so bad about porn in my marriage? Or encouraging my wife to have a little surgery to enhance (or in some cases diminish) her womanly attributes? Why can't I have a little emotional affair? Why can't I have these things if my wife is frumpy or unresponsive or if sex is boring? I can so quickly sink into an attitude of entitlement—I deserve sex (and good sex, at that)—rather than an attitude of gratitude.

Our sexual issues aren't born in a vacuum. They come out of the posture we have toward God. Are we people that focus on the yes, or are we people who obsess on the no?

Idolatry

> Although they claimed to be wise, they became fools and
> exchanged the glory of the immortal God for images
> made to look like mortal man and birds and animals and
> reptiles. Therefore God gave them over in the sinful desires of
> their hearts to sexual impurity for the degrading of their bodies
> with one another. They exchanged the truth of God for a lie,

and worshiped and served created things rather than the Creator—who is forever praised (Romans 1:22-25).

This is the first time Paul mentions sexuality in this chapter. He has been writing the whole time about the readers' view of God. The point is this (and we'll return to this again): Our sexual problems don't start with our bodies and desires. They start with our view of God.

Focusing on the no leads to idolatry. If you focus on what you can't have, you will naturally end up believing (and the enemy will encourage you to believe) God isn't good and that He doesn't have your best interests in mind. Paul says that as this happens, people exchange the glory of God for images and begin to worship created things rather than the Creator who made them.

As we've already said, everyone worships (respects, reveres, turns to) something. We will either worship God or we will turn something else into a god. We can't help it. No one can opt out or abstain. It doesn't matter if you are religious, irreligious, or somewhere in between. We each value and treasure something, and if we trace the path of our time, money, thought, passion, energy, and devotion, we will find what that treasure is.

For many in our culture, the object of worship is sex and desire. In our sex-drenched consumer culture, this is natural. But the Scriptures teach that whatever we worship will bring us under its power. In other words, we become like whatever we worship.[3]

Notice what Paul is saying here: Sex worship is really built on *self* worship. When you give yourself over to sex, you are bowing down to your own wants and desires. "I can't say no" is the epitome of self worship. Paul says that the idol maker becomes the idol itself. You bow down to you, and you can't say anything but yes to your desires. They begin to rule and define and relentlessly lead you further down the path of descent.

Immorality

...sinful desires...sexual impurity...degrading of their bodies with one another...shameful lusts...exchanged natural relations for unnatural ones...inflamed with lust...indecent acts...perversion...depraved mind...every kind of wickedness, evil, greed, and depravity...(Romans 1:24-29).

Paul's list here is pretty condemning. Though not exhaustive, it shows the ways we walk outside God's desires for us. This only happens, though, when we deny the consequences of our actions. Our sexuality provides the most fertile soil for the lies of the enemy and the rationalizations of our heart. A fog settles over our minds when we live apart from God, and our thinking becomes distorted. The more in bondage we are, the more distorted our thinking is. Nowhere do lies more readily multiply than in the area of sex. *If my wife is aloof and unromantic, I am entitled to an emotional affair. If I am alone in a hotel room, I can flip on porn; nobody else will know, and the movie will not appear on the hotel bill. It won't hurt anyone.* Think of all the ways we justify our sin:

We aren't having sex.

No one will know.

Everybody does it.

Men are wired to be visual; porn is a normal part of a sexual man's appetite.

I can look at the menu, as long as I eat at home.

We're only flirting. Emotional affairs aren't real ones.

I deserve this release.

We really are in love.

It will help our marriage.

Our culture doesn't admit this is all nonsense, and most of the time neither does the church. We don't talk about the insidious nature of these temptations, and we don't begin to address the consequences of sexual sin beyond the possibility of pregnancy (though abortion will take care of that) and STDs (and we have great new medications for those). So we go along thinking we won't get caught, it won't hurt when we do, or it just isn't a big deal. Maybe we feel guilty, but biological consequences or emotional guilt aren't the real consequences at all. We may feel bad or not, or we may get sick or not. Either way, what we are doing is the same.

Because of the one-flesh nature of the sex act, we are literally bonding ourselves in deep ways to each other, only to rip away from them and bond with someone else if we sleep around. We leave traces of our souls glued to other people, and we wonder why it is that the more we sin sexually, the less satisfying it becomes. We are shredding our soul's capacity to experience true love and intimacy.

This reminds me of one of the lessons I learned as a boy growing up in the snowy weather of northern Ohio: Never, ever touch your tongue to frozen metal because your tongue will freeze to the metal. The only way to get your tongue unstuck is to pour warm water over it or simply pull yourself away until your tongue rips, leaving a bit of it behind.

This is a picture of what happens during sex. But our health teachers never mentioned that; they told us sex is just a physical issue. But all of us know that isn't true. We know that sex is more than a body thing. Otherwise it wouldn't be a source of such guilt and shame.

When we bond and rip, we reduce our capacity to enjoy the kind of sex and intimacy that God intends for us. Hugh Hefner, the hero of the heterosexual man, embodies the hollowing-out effects of sexual sin. The icon of the carefree and decadent *Playboy* lifestyle no longer can find satisfaction in sex with a woman. Sandy Bentley, a *Playboy* cover girl and former Hefner girlfriend, described his sexual practices: "[He] had trouble finding satisfaction through intercourse; instead he liked the girls to pleasure each other while he masturbated and watched gay porn."[4]

Ours is a culture of slaves telling us they are free. Is this the ultimate in sexual freedom—that we can't even enjoy what God has for us?

Imprisonment

> Therefore God gave them over...Because of this, God gave
> them over...he gave them over...(Romans 1:24,26,28).

We mistake the nature of God's judgment. We think God judges us when sin is exposed—when we get a disease, we get caught in an affair or at the computer, or she gets pregnant—but this is not God's judgment. It is His *mercy!* To be exposed or caught is the kindness of God; God is breaking this cycle and stopping us from sinning further. God shows His love when He stops us from harming ourselves even more.

His judgment is precisely the opposite. We suffer consequences when He does not intervene, when He says, "You can have what you want, and I'll allow it to work fully in your life." We experience God's judgment when He gives us what we think we want. I have learned to pray differently because of this: *Please, stop me! Get in my way! Don't let me have what I am after!*

This is prison: You don't like what you are doing, but you can't stop. When you are given over to something, it rules you. You can't quit. You promise yourself or you promise God that you'll do better the next time, only to find yourself praying that prayer over and over again.

I have known this prison personally, given over to porn, masturbation, and physical relationships with women. I had technical virginity, but I missed entirely what God had in mind. I was given over. That is where I was. God's mercy for me was wrecking my soul to the point where I was so desperate for freedom that I finally told some of my mentors what was really going on. And the power of Jesus was unleashed as I confessed, just as the book of James said it would be.[5]

C.S. Lewis, in *The Lion, the Witch and the Wardrobe*, paints a tragic picture of the slavery of sexual sin. Edmund, one of four siblings who find themselves in the magical land of Narnia, becomes separated from his brother and sisters and is seemingly befriended by a beautiful witch. She curses some Turkish delight so that it is all Edmund wants, but it doesn't satisfy him. The more he eats, the more he wants. The more he eats, the hungrier he gets for it. He would have eaten it until it killed him. It ruined his appetite for anything else.

Always eating, but still getting hungrier. That is the perfect picture of sexual sin. You feel more alienated, alone, empty, and unfulfilled after you do it than before. You don't like it, but you can't stop it and are hungrier after you have gorged yourself. This is the prison Paul talks about. This is what it means to be given over to something.

We can see this happening throughout our culture. For all our sexual prowess and liberation, we see a weary boredom, an almost exhausted numbness that surrounds our images of sex. By reducing sex to genitals, mere technique, and self-serving egoism, and by removing it from the sanctity and mystery of the marriage bed and putting it in the media for all to see, we have profaned sex. It is no longer sacred and mysterious; it is now common and ordinary.

C.S. Lewis again captures the essence of sexual sin in *The Screwtape Letters*. In the book, Screwtape (the devil) explains to his nephew Wormwood the way to tempt humans into sin:

> Never forget that when we are dealing with any pleasure in its healthy and normal and satisfying form, we are, in a sense, on the Enemy's ground. I know we have won many a soul through pleasure. All the same, it is His invention, not ours. He made the pleasures: all our research so far has not enabled us to produce one. All we can do is to encourage the humans to take the pleasures which our Enemy has produced, at times, or in ways, or in degrees which He has forbidden. Hence we always try to work away from the natural condition of any pleasure to that in which it is least natural, least redolent of its Maker, and least pleasurable. An ever increasing craving for an ever diminishing pleasure is the formula.[6]

Sin is that way. We once had a choice, but now we have a near compulsion. Each new generation enters a world that has long ago lost its Eden, a world that is now half ruined by the billions of bad choices and millions of old habits congealed into thousands of cultures across the ages.

Nothing about God's commands is arbitrary. He protects us for our good. The descent described leads to this masculine sexual condition: Against all reason, we continue to choose against what's good for us. We live in opposition to God and others (and even ourselves). Choices we made when we were younger have turned into habits and addictions that now have led to a slavery that is beyond our power to escape.

But we have hope. "God is not a warden; He is a deliverer."[7] He has come to set us free from the things that enslave us. Yes, He died to forgive us. But Jesus also died to set us free.[8] I have come to know this hope firsthand. There really is a way out; you don't have to be trapped in the darkness of sexual sin forever.

Chapter 9

WALKING DOWN ANOTHER STREET

In accepting what God wills for us do we find our peace.

Dante Alighieri

Sex is good. It is powerful. And when it comes to sex, most of us find ourselves somewhere on the spiral downward from ingratitude to imprisonment. But we can find freedom at any step of the way by being honest about our sexual issues and struggles.[1]

Where Do You Find Yourself?

Most likely, you found yourself described somewhere in the last couple of chapters. When we talk of sex and sexuality, we must remind ourselves constantly that our sexual issues began with our view of God. Healing does not come through you feeling more ashamed of yourself. Freedom does not come from trying harder. Healing comes through figuring out where this began and then cutting it off at the root. The problem began with ingratitude—a basic orientation toward life that leads us to independence and entitlement. This has to change in us; we must reorient ourselves toward God and change our posture to one of humble dependence and thankfulness. Once we change that, sexuality will find its place.

Either I walk around as a grateful person, thankful for my life, or I walk around complaining and whining, focused on what I don't have. There really is no third option. Think about how much we complain. If we are single, we are bummed that we can't have sex, or we are focused on our loneliness. If we are married, we want sex more often, or we are bored with our spouse and wonder what it would be like to have sex with someone else. We complain about most everything. At the core, most of us are not grateful people.

I can't be grateful unless I see myself as small, dependent, and undeserving. I know that reorienting myself this way doesn't feel manly. But we will never experience healing and victory over sexual struggles as long as our posture toward God is one of entitlement.

This is fundamental. Have I adopted a posture of entitlement before God and placed my sexuality within that (God made me this way, so I need to have sex), or am I cultivating a thankful heart and focusing on the incredible yes God has given me? If I see His blessing in the yes, then I can trust Him on the no. If I live focused on all I do have instead of what I don't have, I become the kind of person who isn't as easily tempted by the empty promises of the world around me.

Maybe entitlement isn't your issue, but the idea that your desires rule you resonates with your heart. Perhaps, in some way, you bow down to *you:* You can't say no to what you want, and you have made desire king of your life. When you want it, you get it, whether it's gadgets, toys, tools, or sex. Perhaps your whole life is centered on your desires and wants, and you spend your energy trying to fulfill them. If this is the case, God is asking you to put Him in His rightful place in your life. Maybe your sexual issues come from bowing down to you instead of to Him. Sexual sin is really an issue of worship, so perhaps healing and freedom could come from accepting that God really has our good in mind and that we don't always know what is best for us.

Or perhaps you are like me—great at minimizing or justifying sexual sin. I like to play a game called Big Sins, Small Sins. I make an unbiblical (but thoroughly convenient) distinction between big sins (rape, murder, theft) and small sins (lust, porn, masturbation) and rationalize my indulgence in the small sins by reminding myself that I'm better than the guys committing the big sins. I usually label whatever I'm currently struggling with as a small sin, and one of God's mercies to me is blowing those minimizations and justifications out of the water. Perhaps healing and forgiveness find us when we begin to get honest and recognize our sin for what it is.

Many of us also feel as if we're in a prison. Maybe that is where you are right now. Or maybe you can remember how that used to feel. How can we break free? Is it just a matter of trying harder? Where do we find healing?

Where We Go from Here

As we have said many times, the first and most important step toward healing and restoration is honesty. God can restore us to what He intended for us in the first place. He forgives us, but He also does much more. He brings light where there was darkness, truth where there was deceit, freedom where there was slavery, and forgiveness where there was shame and guilt. To live honestly, we must fight through our justifications, minimizations, and rationalizing and admit we are wrong. This is a big deal. Too much of church and religion entices us to hide and pretend. We think God can't (or won't) handle our stuff when we bring it to Him.

But the process of freedom starts when we acknowledge our issues before God and others, admit weakness and struggle, and come clean about the ways we have been pretending and hiding. For most men, this is a brutal process. We are forced to wear many stupid cultural masks that make coming clean difficult.

The word the Bible uses for coming clean is *confession*. It means to agree with God's view of our actions and attitudes—that they are sin. We don't hide or diminish what we have done; we simply are honest about how God sees it.

This was true for me; I needed to let someone else know the secrets of my inner life. Trusted friends, family, or mentors are needed here. We strip away all of our lies and justifications and simply allow someone else into the ugliness of what we have been doing. Secrecy gives this stuff its power. Once we come clean and recognize that so many men have these same struggles and so many have seen God's power in overcoming them, we stand ready to begin the process of reorienting our lives toward what is healthy and good.

I know this is uncomfortable, but what do we really want? If you enjoy prison, by all means, go ahead and stay there. But confession is the way of Jesus and the way of the cross. This sin must die, both in action and in attitude, before we can taste new life. Shame loves the darkness and will die when brought out into the light.

Pretending and hiding never lead to freedom. I love how James puts it: "Therefore confess your sins to each other and pray for each other so that you may be healed" (James 5:16).

As we bring this stuff out into the light before God and some trustworthy men, we begin to discover God's grace and mercy.[2] He has forgiven us in Christ. He has known about our sin all along but has loved us anyway. As people around us begin to put flesh and blood on this—when they hear about our sin and love and accept us anyway—we begin to learn that pretending to be something we aren't will never lead us to freedom. Only by coming clean do we begin that journey.

Confession, then, isn't a one-time thing; it is a lifestyle.[3] We learn to quit pretending. We learn that there is a God and there are people who will still love us when we really let them in. This is an ongoing process of learning to live without posturing and pretending. As we begin to admit our powerlessness over the struggles of our lives apart from Christ, we begin to walk in our new identity as followers of Him.[4] We can begin again (and again and again); that is the good news of Jesus. He has not abandoned us to ourselves. Yes, there are consequences to our sin, but we are not damaged goods. The cross of Jesus has done away with guilt and shame.

Sometimes we refuse to confess. We keep denying our sin or distracting ourselves from it. We fail to acknowledge what we have done wrong. David (a pretty big sinner from the Old Testament) writes about what happens when we keep hiding and do not come clean:

> Blessed is he whose transgressions are forgiven, whose sins are covered. Blessed is the man whose sin the LORD does not count against him and in whose spirit is no deceit. When I kept silent [about my sin], my bones wasted away through my groaning all day long. For day and night your hand was heavy upon me; my strength was sapped as in the heat of summer. Then I acknowledged my sin to you and did not cover up my inequity. I said, "I will confess my transgressions to the LORD"—and you forgave the guilt of my sin (Psalm 32:1-5).

David is saying that God's blessing and goodness rests on those who come clean and quit hiding. We must start by coming clean. We are no longer going to pretend this is okay. This doesn't mean that we deny that we are confident and gifted. It just means that we quit acting as if our strengths are the only things true of us.

God isn't the only one who plays a part in our healing and restoration; we have a role to play as well. We are called to repentance. This is a strong word that means to turn around or to go back to where we belong. It is the way that we push away the sin that so easily entangles us. Repentance includes the idea of making restitution—not only agreeing that we messed up and made a mistake but also trying to return things to how they should be.[5]

I have sat with many men (and have been one myself) who genuinely grieve their slavery to sexual sin, confess it to God and others, and wonder why they have not been set free. When pressed for details, many of them will often admit that their computer is still next to their bed, or they are driving the same way to work (right past that massage parlor), or that they are still flirting with the married woman in the corner office. God will not do our part for us. We must grow desperate enough to cancel cable television, trash the computer, or break the illicit relationship. I have found power in this. This is repentance.

God is looking for a certain response to fallenness and sin. Here was David's confession:

> Have mercy on me, O God, according to your unfailing love; according to your great compassion blot out my transgressions. Wash away all my iniquity and cleanse me from my sin.
>
> For I know my transgressions, and my sin is always before me. Against you, you only, have I sinned and done what is evil in your sight, so that you are proved right when you speak and justified when you judge. Surely I was sinful at birth, sinful from the time my mother conceived me...
>
> Cleanse me with hyssop, and I will be clean; wash me, and I will be whiter than snow...Create in me a pure heart, O God, and renew a steadfast spirit within me...Restore to me the joy of your salvation and grant me a willing spirit, to sustain me...
>
> O Lord, open my lips, and my mouth will declare your praise. You do not delight in sacrifice, or I would bring it; you do not take pleasure in burnt offerings. The sacrifices of God are a broken spirit; a broken and contrite heart, O God, you will not despise.[6]

We are humble and contrite when we come out of hiding and confess what we've done, and then we're grateful to receive forgiveness. This, in turn, leads us to repentance.[7] We can do nothing to earn God's love and approval, so we are now free to respond to Him out of gratitude. Confession is only part of the story. Yes, we are forgiven when we confess, but if we do not turn away from the things causing us to fall, we are still hardening and numbing our heart and forming our soul around these desires.

We don't do this alone. We can't, and we don't have to. We recognize the spiritual battle taking place over our purity of mind and body. We are powerless to fight the battle in our own strength. By calling on the name of Jesus, and by His authority, blood, and cross, we engage the enemy and rebuke the lies that give power to sexual strongholds.[8]

One of these lies is that we are not truly forgiven. We must hold on to the Scriptures that promise us that our sin has been dismissed. Not only that, but the Scriptures teach we are declared pure and clean and that we have received God's power to live new lives. The same power that raised Jesus from the dead now lives in us through God's Spirit. Unless we depend on God's strength while doing our part in the process of repentance, our temptations will continue to pull at us even if we succeed at avoiding them. As we begin to live more and more this way (deliberately dependent on God's strength instead of our own), those things that cause us to struggle eventually become unexciting and unattractive. We begin to desire for ourselves the things God wants for us.

We also have another part to play. Are you tired of being enslaved to porn? Toss your computer. Marriage is disappointing? Start marital counseling. Can't say no to your girlfriend? Break up with her. This is how ruthless we must be. I am inspired by a couple in our church who were once divorced. When they began studying these truths, God started an amazing work in them. They dedicated themselves to purity, began to receive counseling, and started walking the very difficult road of restoration. They are now married again, have since become parents, and are filled with joy.

Outside of real-life examples, here is the best picture of repentance I have ever seen:

> There's a Hole in My Sidewalk—an Autobiography in Five Short Chapters
>
> Chapter One
>
> I walk down the street. There is a deep hole in the sidewalk. I fall in. I am lost...I am helpless. It isn't my fault. It takes forever to find a way out.
>
> Chapter Two
>
> I walk down the street. There is a deep hole in the sidewalk. I pretend that I don't see it. I fall in again. I can't believe that I

am in this same place. But, it isn't my fault. It still takes a long time to get out.

Chapter Three

I walk down the same street. There is a deep hole in the sidewalk. I see it is there. I still fall in...it's a habit...but my eyes are open. I know where I am. It is my fault. I get out immediately.

Chapter Four

I walk down the same street. There is a deep hole in the sidewalk. I walk around it.

Chapter Five

I walk down another street.[9]

Walking down another street means that I start to live differently. Our world tells us this isn't possible. Jesus tells us we can change the way we live and that there is another street to walk down. Paul implies this in 1 Corinthians 10:13:

No temptation has seized you except what is common to man. And God is faithful: he will not let you be tempted beyond what you can bear. But when you are tempted, he will also provide a way out so that you can stand up under it.

One of the great lies of our culture is that we can't control our sexual feelings. That isn't true, of course. Just because I am sexually attracted to many people doesn't mean that I have to sleep with them, just as my being mad at lots of people doesn't mean I am going to punch them. I don't have to punch others, and I don't have to sleep with them. In Christ, I simply do not have to live according to my whims.

This lie, though, is nothing new. In 1 Corinthians 6:12, Paul begins to quote a series of statements the Corinthians used to justify doing anything they wanted:

"Everything is permissible for me"—but not everything is beneficial. "Everything is permissible for me"—but I will not be mastered by anything. "Food for the stomach and the stomach for food"—but God will destroy them both. The body is not meant for sexual immorality, but for the Lord, and the Lord for the body...Do you not know that your bodies are members of Christ himself? Shall I then take the members of Christ and unite them with a prostitute? Never! Do you not know that he who unites himself with a prostitute is one with her in body? For it is said, "The two will become one flesh." But he who unites himself with the Lord is one with him in spirit. Flee from sexual immorality. All other sins a man commits are outside his body, but he who sins sexually sins against his own body. Do you not know that your body is a temple of the Holy Spirit, who is in you, whom you have received from God? You are not your own; you were bought at a price. Therefore honor God with your body.

The Corinthians entertained an idea that their bodies and their spirits were completely unconnected. They believed they could do whatever they wanted with their body and that their soul would remain untouched. "Food for the stomach and the stomach for food," they said. It meant two things. First, the separation between our bodies and our souls would leave the soul unaffected when the body followed its desires. Second, like the need for food, our need for sex should be allowed for the same reasons. We have human physical needs that demand satisfaction. Food is one, and the Corinthians believed sex was another.

They were a culture of slaves who said they were free. So are we. Our culture teaches us that we are helpless against our urges. ("The kids are going to have sex, so we had better give them condoms.")

But Paul counters this idea in two ways. First, he reminds us of the connection between body and soul. One does affect the other. Particularly in the area of sex, we use our whole person (body, mind, heart, soul) in the act. Yes, we have basic human needs for survival, but the Corinthians had taken a phrase and applied it to all sorts of other physical urges that were not needs. I have yet to hear of someone who died from a lack of sex.

Joshua Harris comments on this issue:

> Keep this radical and liberating idea in mind: God wants you to embrace your sexuality—battling lust is a part of that. Does that sound contradictory? That is because our culture offers a very narrow definition of what it means to embrace sexuality—it equates embracing your sexuality with doing whatever feels good. So according to our culture, to deny a sexual impulse at any point is to be untrue to yourself. As followers of Jesus, embracing sexuality looks different: we don't obey every sexual impulse—nor do we deny we have sexual desires. Instead, we choose restraint and gratefulness—for us, sexual desire joins every other part of our lives—appetites for food, use of money, dreams, friendships, possessions, abilities—in bowing before the one true God.[10]

Second, Paul reminds us that we live for more than the simple meeting of physical desire. There is more to life, Paul says, than indulging our urges and needs. He calls us to something more in life (and to see our bodies as more than simply a bundle of physical desires) when he declares that "your body is a temple of the Holy Spirit, who is in you, whom you have received from God" (1 Corinthians 6:19). This language is dramatic. The temple in the Old Testament was the place where God dwelt with His people. To say that our bodies are now temples was to recognize that Jesus had accomplished something in us that had deep implications. The way that we would treat God's temple is the way we should treat our bodies.

Who We Become

Freedom, healing, and hope are available for those of us caught up in the misuse of sexual desire.[11] We begin by learning how to deal with the guilt and shame of sexual failure. Far too many men have been shipwrecked by the idea that they are disqualified from being fruitful for God because of their sexual past (or present). John Piper refers to this:

The great tragedy is not mainly masturbation or fornication or acting like a peeping Tom (or curious Cathy) on the internet. The tragedy is that Satan uses the guilt of these failures to strip you of every radical dream you ever had, or might have, and in its place give you a happy, safe, secure, American life.[12]

We need to understand the magnitude of the work of Jesus on our behalf and get used to the idea that we are clean, pure, holy, and righteous in His eyes.[13] One of the clearest pictures of the work of Jesus is in Colossians 2:13-14:

When you were dead in your sins and in the uncircumcision of your sinful nature, God made you alive with Christ. He forgave us all our sins, having canceled the written code, with its regulations, that was against us and that stood opposed to us; he took it away, nailing it to the cross.

What an amazing picture. We imagine a list of all the sins (including our sexual failures, fantasies, indulgences, and jokes) that could be used to condemn us. The list is nailed to the cross with Jesus. He satisfied God's justice by taking upon Himself the punishment we should have received. Instead of waving that list in our face, God has dispensed with it altogether.

So confession and repentance lead us to understand the most liberating thought imaginable: The sin and failure in my life no longer define the way God sees me. Nowhere in the New Testament are believers in Jesus called sinners. Instead, we are called saints, ministers, priests, and sons. This is our new identity.[14] Our lives are now swallowed up with Jesus in God, and though the old self rears its ugly head and leads us to sin, that is no longer who we fundamentally are.[15] Each of us is a new creation in Christ; the image of God in us that has been tarnished and broken by sin is now restored. If the image is restored in Christ, when God looks at us, He sees somebody else. He sees Jesus and not how fallen we have been.

That is why dealing with sexual sin isn't usually an overnight fix. We need a different view of God (which leads to gratitude), ourselves (we are saints, not sinners), women (more about that in a couple of chapters), sex (it is important, but only secondarily so; it is not the most important thing about us or our masculinity), and our bodies (they are temples of the Holy Spirit). Nothing short of the work of God can bring about these changes in us.

Our sexual struggles are often part of other issues—anger, pride, selfishness, loneliness, worry, stress, the need for love and acceptance—so we recognize that we need to grow in wholeness as men, not just in the area of sexuality.[16]

Recognizing and living out our new identity requires sustained grace from God and a change in the basic direction and aim of life. None of this is a one-time practice; none of it is a quick fix. But hope is the issue. God created us for Eden, and in Christ, He has restored our ability to be naked and unashamed.

I read a section heading in a book that describes our current situation perfectly: "Truly changed, truly changing, and still at war." That is where we find ourselves. We are truly changed into new beings when we identify ourselves with Jesus Christ. We are truly changing more and more into looking like Jesus. And we are still at war. The enemy of our hearts wants nothing more than for men to spend their lives either pursuing sexual gratification or punishing themselves for sexual failure. The way of Jesus provides a third way: the way of forgiveness, healing, and restoration. With Him, all things are possible.

Part Four

IN THE ARENA

Chapter 10

BAND OF BROTHERS AND SISTERS

> We continue to walk the path to maturity when we admit
> how deeply we long for a father, a man who walks ahead
> of us, letting us know what is possible and calling us to
> follow; and a brother, a peer whose struggles and compas-
> sion encourage us to make ourselves known to him as we
> walk together. When the reality hits us, as it will for most
> men, that we have neither father nor brother, the over-
> whelming disappointment can either turn into bitterness
> or it can drive us to seek God with all our hearts and to
> become fathers and brothers for other men.
>
> LARRY CRABB

When we examine the early chapters of Genesis, we see God's intent for men to live in community with others. This is part of what it means to be human. As we have seen, to be made in God's image means that we reflect central features of what God is like. The ability and need to relate to other human beings are essential parts of that likeness. This is obvious, but what is not so obvious is what this means for men thousands of years later.

The Christian idea of the Trinity takes a little getting used to. In essence, it is the belief that God is triune in His nature. This means that God, who exists as one essence, also exists as three persons. This is easy to say but hard to wrap our minds around.[1] Many Christians assume the idea is simply a New Testament concept. But we actually see the first inklings of that doctrine in the opening pages of Genesis.

We find this idea in the first three verses of the Bible. In Genesis 1:1, God created the heavens and the earth. In the next verse, we read of the Spirit of God hovering over the waters. And in verse 3, God speaks creation into existence using words. It is no coincidence that Jesus is called the Word in John 1:1-3: "In the beginning [note the Genesis language] was the Word, and the Word was with God, and the Word was God...Through him all things were made; without him nothing was made that has been made."

So we have one God who is present in three distinct ways: God the Creator, God the Spirit, and God the Word. Notice also that the word used for God in Genesis 1:1, *Elohim,* is a plural noun. In the Hebrew language, any word ending in *im* is the equivalent of adding an *ies* to an English word to change it from being singular to plural. Though this doesn't prove the doctrine of the Trinity, it does suggest that there is plurality within the Godhead.

Looking back at the full revelation of God through both the Hebrew Scriptures and the New Testament, we can trace the development of the idea of God being three in one. Or, as one friend put it, God is one "what" and three "whos"—one essence shared by three distinct persons.[2]

Even the clearest Jewish text declaring the oneness of God has trinitarian theology behind it: "Hear, O Israel: The LORD our God, the LORD is one. Love the LORD your God with all your heart and with all your soul and with all your strength" (Deuteronomy 6:4-5). The word for "one" is *echad,* and it denotes not an absolute unity but rather a composite unity (one thing that is made up of several parts). The same word is used in Genesis 2 where two people "become one *[echad]* flesh." Because of the unity of the two, we may speak of them as one, yet they retain their individual identity. They are two and one at the same time.

Despite Jewish objections to the contrary, there are hints of the unique nature of God found all throughout the Old Testament.[3] And it is seen in the New Testament as well, most clearly at the baptism of Jesus.[4] The earliest proclamations of the first century church declared Jesus to be God in human form, and the practice of baptism was done in the name of the Father, Son, and Holy Spirit.[5] Jesus also spoke of the life He had with the Father before He was incarnated: "And now, Father, glorify me in your presence with the glory I had with you before the world began" (John 17:5).

The idea of the Trinity was present in the ministry of Jesus and in the life of the early church, and it continues to be a central doctrine to this day.[6]

> The Creator himself contains, within himself, a multiple relationship...We do indeed know that we were made for relationships and that we find relationships difficult...The call to relationship, and the sad rebuke for our failures at it, can be heard together as echoes of a voice...We can already tell enough about that voice that we would know its owner if we met it. Its owner would be one who was totally committed to relationships of every sort—with other human beings, with the Creator, with the natural world. And yet that owner would share the pain of the brokenness of each of these relationships. One of the central elements of the Christian story is the claim that the paradox of laughter and tears, woven as it is deep into the heart of all human experience, is woven also deep into the heart of God.[7]

God lives and exists in a community of self-giving love. He didn't create us because He was lonely, bored, or desperate for someone to worship Him. His joy and love overflow into His creation. We see this at the very beginning of our story. And if we are made in the image of God, it follows that we share in this central part of Him. We long for what it is that God Himself enjoys. The fact that we are made in the image of a triune God explains why we are so hungry for deep and real connection with others and why we so earnestly desire to be known, accepted, and respected. It explains why so much of our art, music, poetry, and media are devoted to friendship, relationship, and love. Why do we love TV shows like *Friends, Seinfeld,* and *Cheers?* We can't help but connect with others. It is who we are and how we were made.

This is why we will always take technology that isolates and use it subversively to connect. My Xbox, cell phone, personal computer—all could be instruments of isolation, yet they become places of connection between others. We have an instinctive need to know and be known. Why do we talk on the phone all the time? Or text? Or e-mail? We can't help it. All of this goes back before there were any people to begin with. This is not primarily a Christian thing; it is a human thing.

This also explains why male and female are never defined apart from their relationship to each other. We are brought into relationship with God through Jesus, but instead of ending there, Jesus leads us into new sorts of relationships. The New Testament ethic assumes such community, and our own experience validates it.

The picture presented in the earliest chapters of Genesis is of a man and a woman in perfect harmony and peace with God, each other, and the rest of creation. This is what we were made for and what Jesus later calls us back into.

Interestingly, not everything was considered good in the Garden of Eden. One thing was wrong even before sin entered the world. The powerful refrain of Genesis 1—"It was good"—is interrupted in chapter 2 when God looks at the man and declares, "It is not good for the man to be alone. I will make a helper suitable for him" (Genesis 2:18).[8] This was pre-fall, before sin entered the world. Adam was not able to fully reflect the image of God without Eve.

This has important implications for us as men. There is a teaching in Christian circles that goes something like this: "All you need is God. If you are lonely, pray. If you are depressed or anxious, read the Bible more. He is all you need." In one sense, this is true. He is sufficient to meet all our needs. And certainly prayer and Bible reading are tremendously important disciplines. But God Himself doesn't say, "All you need is Me." In fact, He says just the opposite to Adam.

This idea that I am not supposed to need anybody else is not found in the Bible. Adam had God to himself in the garden—no sin, no shame, no fear—just God. And yet God declared that he needed someone else. It is not good to be alone. That was true for Adam; it is true for us.[9] Man's aloneness was an impediment to his complete fulfillment; we need more than a solitary experience of God. God made us with certain needs that are intrinsic to being human, needs that only a fellow human can meet.

How many times does God speak to us through others? Or comfort us? Convict us? Encourage us? I have a group of friends that I call the "two o'clock in the morning crew." These are guys that I can call anytime, day or night, if I need help. I don't know what I would have done without them. There have been times these guys have kept me on the straight and narrow, or brought encouragement when I was down, or simply sat with me when I was anxious or depressed. I have learned from these guys that two of the most powerful words we men can say to each other are "me too." As I have walked the journey to wholeness and healing, these guys were essential in my learning that I was not alone and that God was present.

This isn't optional stuff. Though we may try to live without these kinds of relationships, we crave this depth of connection. Many of us, however, find this level of authentic relationship daunting or unmanly, or we may just not know how to find, build, or keep it. This is because our natural inclination is to hide behind our fig leaves.

Into Hiding

Genesis 1–2 portrays two people who are totally themselves, who have nothing to hide, and who live in perfect intimacy. Blame, shame, guilt, and fear are simply unknown. Nothing stands in the way of their connection. They know each other and accept each other fully. Once they disobey, however, a fascinating thing happens:

> When the woman saw that the fruit of the tree was good for food and pleasing to the eye, and also desirable for gaining wisdom, she took some and ate it. She also gave some to her husband, who was with her, and he ate it. Then the eyes of both of them were opened, and they realized they were naked; so they sewed fig leaves together and made coverings for themselves.
>
> Then the man and his wife heard the sound of the LORD God as he was walking in the garden in the cool of the day, and they hid from the LORD God among the trees of the garden. But the LORD God called to the man, "Where are you?" He answered, "I heard you in the garden, and I was afraid because I was naked; so I hid."
>
> And he said, "Who told you that you were naked? Have you eaten from the tree that I commanded you not to eat from?" The man said, "The woman you put here with me—she gave me some fruit from the tree, and I ate it." Then the LORD God said to the woman, "What is this you have done?" The woman said, "The serpent deceived me, and I ate" (Genesis 3:6-13).

The moment Adam and Eve live outside of God's intent for them, what is the first thing affected? Their relationships with each other and with God. This again reminds us of how central relationships are. Adam and Eve go from naked and unashamed to naked and ashamed in the blink of an eye. They become aware of themselves in a way they weren't previously. They realize they are naked, so their first inclination is to cover up and hide.

This is the first thing we are told about the results of taking the fruit. Sin appears first in their relationships. They don't hijack a car or anything, but they withdraw from each other. Innocence and vulnerability were replaced with fear and blame.

Our problems with each other are as old as humanity itself. The universal masculine response to sin, failure, fear, and shame is to hide behind our fig leaves. We believe the lie that if people really knew us, they wouldn't love or respect us. We don't feel as if we can let people in on who we really are, or they will leave us.

So, like Adam, we go into hiding. Our fig leaves are nothing new. They are all around us. Our fig leaves are a little more creative these days, but they serve the same purpose. Whether we use success, money, status, accomplishment, passivity, anger, or indulgence, the result is the same: We find something to cover with or hide behind. I am terrified of what would happen if people saw all the stuff that is true of me. Now restraint, distance, mistrust, and antagonism characterize human relationships. This isn't a religious problem; it is a human problem.

Out of Hiding

We were created for deep, authentic community and relationship, but our fig leaves get in the way. One of the purposes of the church is to help us put them away and come out of hiding. The people of God are called, again and again, to be a safe haven where people can be real. If they do this well, they can literally put hands and feet (or mouths and ears) to God's love for us.

As a pastor, I hear some really deep stuff from people during our weekend services. Many times men will share something huge with me that is going on in their lives. I usually ask them who else they have told about this, and I am no longer surprised to hear that they haven't told anyone else. They carry horrible, gut-wrenching stuff all by themselves. This is not how it should be. It is not good for man to be alone.

The New Testament is full of directives that can make the church an honest place where people can come out of hiding. These are often called the "one anothers" of the Bible—commands given to Christians about how they should treat one another. There are over 40 of them, including these:

- Be kind to one another.
- Encourage one another.

- Be patient with one another.

- Love one another.

- Devote yourselves to one another.

- Spur one another on to love and good deeds.

- Confess your sins to one another and pray for one another.

- Build one another up.

- Forgive one another.

All of these assume the messiness of human relationships. When we come out of hiding in front of each other, relationship will take hard work and lots of grace. The church gets a lot of criticism because of its imperfections. I have been told countless times about how our church wasn't welcoming or friendly, but what else should we expect from a bunch of work-in-progress reformed sinners? Ronald Rolheiser is realistic about this:

> To be connected with the church is to be associated with scoundrels, warmongers, fakes, child-molesters, murderers, adulterers, and hypocrites of every description. It also, at the same time, identifies you with saints and the finest persons of heroic soul within every time, country, race, and gender. To be a member of the church is to carry the mantle of both the worst sin and the finest heroism of the soul...because the church always looks exactly as it looked at the original crucifixion: God hung among thieves.[10]

This is why the pretentiousness of much of the American church is so damaging. Most churches teach men how to pretend behind religious fig leaves.[11] We learn to act in the right religious ways, look the right religious ways, sing the right religious ways, and so on. We usually are not encouraged to actually share how things really are. So even though we need to connect with other guys at a really deep level, the church often actually hinders this process.

Being religious is actually the best way to keep our fig leaves on. We may think that immorality, materialism, or the hunger for success is the most likely candidate for that honor, but I am no longer sure. Jesus repeatedly warned the religious men of His day against missing who He was because of their own religiousness.[12] Jesus spent a lot of time teaching the good people that they weren't as good as they thought and teaching the bad people they were not as far away from God as they thought.

We need to hear Jesus' message today. Many of us are lulled into comfortable mediocrity by constantly reassuring ourselves that we are better than the next guy, and (though we would never put it this way) we secretly think God is lucky to have us on His team. By playing the religion/church game, we can avoid actually encountering God or sharing our real selves with others.

I will never forget a teacher friend of mine telling our church staff one day, "Prayer isn't a place to be good; it is a place to be honest."[13] These words were so liberating precisely because prayer (and worship, and everything else about God) had become places for me to perform and to earn the approval of God and men. I had ceased being honest with God, and my prayer life became a series of clichés that I only half meant.

Freedom and healing have come for me when I have turned away from trying to impress everyone (including God) and started being honest. I know this is simple, but I found living authentically harder than I'd imagined it to be. One of the scariest things for a man to do is to ask someone for help and admit weakness in front of another. This is brutal but necessary. I can distinctly remember being upset by something a friend had said but not wanting to tell him for fear of being seen as petty because the issue was small. I was getting ready for work one morning when the thought hit me, *I AM small!* I told my friend what was bothering me, we patched things up, and one fig leaf was removed. In little ways and big ones, I am learning this is a lifelong journey.

Boys in Men's Bodies

Men's need to hide is especially acute because of the epidemic of fatherlessness in the Western world. We'll look at some mind-numbing statistics in a couple of chapters. There are many reasons why the emotional and/or physical absence of fathers is so devastating, but we will highlight only one. As many have pointed out, masculinity is bestowed; that is, we are born male, but only a community of other men can define us as men.[14]

> In almost all cultures men are not born; they are made. Much more than for women, cultures have traditionally demanded initiation rites specifically for the boys. It is almost as if the biological experiences of menstruation and childbirth are enough wisdom lessons for women, but invariably men must be tried, limited, challenged, punished, hazed, circumcised, isolated, starved, stripped, and goaded into masculinity. The pattern is nearly universal...For men, the issue of father leaves a huge aching void inside that is never really filled. They grow up without a good man's love, without a father's understanding and affirmation. So they hunger for it, and they search for it from teachers and coaches, ministers and scoutmasters, and any older man who will offer it to them. Later, in the military or business world, they seek to be approved by their superiors in exactly the same way. They will do anything for the comfort and assurance that "Daddy's" approval gives them.[15]

If it is true that other men bestow masculinity on us, then growing up without good dads hurts us far deeper than we'd imagined. We have had no one to guide us on the way through the masculine journey. Who will show us what it means to be a man, husband, father, worker, friend, lover, and disciple if our dads didn't?

The media and Hollywood do their best to fill this void, but their images of masculinity are neither believable nor livable for those of us who are honest with ourselves. We long for guides at every stage of the masculine journey; we want to know that it is possible to stay married in a divorce-happy culture, to find success without compromising integrity, or to be a follower of Jesus without turning into a soft guy. Fatherlessness hurts us precisely because we need someone to guide us into masculinity. And if our dads can't (or won't, or weren't around enough to try), then we look elsewhere.

Since we are without masculine affirmation from our fathers, we look to other men for this assurance and acceptance. The gang phenomenon bears this out. Having no men in their lives who give them a healthy sense of confidence in who they are, gang members are constantly trying to prove themselves—to each other, but also to themselves. They engage in deadly games of physical fitness, violence, sexual prowess, or business success because they desperately need to know that they are really men. But their continuous running from one accomplishment to another only proves that they have not yet made it to the only place that really counts. Their constant search for worth betrays their inner sense of worthlessness.

Having no guide along the road to masculinity cripples us into hiding. We have to perform, one way or another, to be loved and accepted. We find some level of safety behind our fig leaves. Coming out of hiding is terrifying because we've never been given permission to be ourselves. So we walk around as "unfinished men," boys who have men's bodies but who have never grown up on the inside. Our desperation for affirmation clouds our vision and compels us to counterfeits: sexual encounters, alcohol, endless TV ball games, overworking, legalistic religion...the list of compulsive efforts to save ourselves from shame is as long as a man's natural energy allows.

The community of Jesus must become more than simply the place we go once a week to worship God. It must become the family of God, full of spiritual fathers and mothers, brothers and sisters. This image, found all over the New Testament, is one for our time. Jesus Himself declared our bonds with others in His kingdom to be far more important than the biological bonds that tie us to our families.[16]

Obviously, God Himself must become our Father, and we need to begin to find our sense of worth, identity, and value from Him.[17] We are His sons and have been adopted into His family.[18] Many of us never knew the happiness and security of being a son who was greatly loved by his father and made safe and secure by his presence in our lives. God desires to give us that security, but He cannot apart from our involvement in the community of faith.

We are not independent people. We live in a whole web of dependencies, not only on God but also on a community of people. We were created to know the intimacy and relationship that God Himself enjoys. So we must become people who live with God and others in ways that bring out the good and bad in us. Marriage may help this, but it is not sufficient by itself. Nor are business acquaintances or friendships built solely on common interests. No, we must reach deeper if we are to find the life that Jesus has for us. We must seek out guides and mentors, comrades and teammates, and some who are behind us in the journey for us to lead as we go—all the while keeping in view the affirmation and affection that a loving God has toward us.

This is not easy, quick, or painless, but it is well worth the effort. Only in relationship to others do we find ourselves. Only in dependence, weakness, humility, and honesty do we realize that we don't have to pretend, hide, or posture. We are affirmed as we are, warts and all, and the central work of God's Spirit within us is to help us discover that is true.

Chapter 11

POWER AND CONTROL

The ideology of masculinity has replaced Christianity as the true religion of men. We live in a society with a female religion and a male religion: Christianity, of various sorts, for women and non-masculine men; and masculinity, especially in the forms of competition and violence that culminate in war, for men.

LEON J. PODLES

My wife and I don't argue often, but when we do, we go all out. We have been married for more than seven years and have noticed a curious pattern to our fights. Usually one of us will be upset about something the other did or said and then comment on how we were hurt by what was done. That part is all fine and good. But we never stay there. We typically broaden the issue to include other stuff. Let's say (hypothetically, of course) that I forgot to do something around the house. My sweetie will be hurt by my thoughtlessness and express that hurt, but then she will broaden the issue to include her general desire that I were more sensitive to how messy our house gets with two kids. (She's sensitive to how messy our house gets with two kids.) I will bristle at the implication that I am failing her as a husband, so I will counter with my wish that she verbally affirmed me more. (I'm always verbally affirming her.) She will respond by pointing out that she would love it if I did stuff for her without being asked. (She does stuff for me all the time without being asked.) I tell her that I can't read her mind, so she should communicate her expectations to me. (I communicate my expectations to her all the time.) And on it goes. What happened to the thing I forgot to do? It gets buried under all the other stuff we got into.

Do you see what has happened to us? I have noticed that our fights mostly center on me trying to get my wife to be more like me and my wife trying to get me to be more like her. Instead of delighting in our differences and tolerating our weaknesses, we try to pound the other person into our own image. Things would be better if my wife were more like me (or I more like her), or so we believe.

Once you notice this conflict, it seems to exist everywhere we look. To some degree, we feel this way toward our friends, our roommates, our kids, our parents, our siblings, our coworkers, and the guy in front of us on the road.

This sort of dynamic between husbands and wives specifically (or men and women generally) is certainly nothing new. It is as old as humanity itself. In chapter 4, we looked at the judgments and curses handed down by God in response to the sin of Adam and Eve. Though God made men (and women) to experience deep relational connection and intimacy (with Himself and with others) as part of His good design, our own sin and the judgments of Genesis 3 have made that difficult. You'll recall with me the judgment on the woman: "To the woman he said, 'I will greatly increase your pains in childbearing; with pain you will give birth to children. Your desire will be for your husband, and he will rule over you'" (Genesis 3:16).

We must understand two words in this verse in order to glimpse the reality of this judgment. The word translated *rule* means to dominate, to keep beneath, to rule over as an absolute sovereign. The word is used of kings and public officials throughout the Old Testament. This is a statement of curse, not kingdom; of judgment, not design. Those who use this verse to justify male domination miss its point entirely. This passage foretells how fallen men will naturally tend to treat their wives. They will dominate them and subjugate them to positions of lower status. Men will want to treat their wives as second-class citizens and enrich themselves at the expense of women. We have thousands of cultures and years to document that this is exactly what has taken place.

The word translated *desire* here is also interesting. The way the sentence is structured, the desire of the woman is set against the rule of the man. Several suggestions have been made about what *desire* means, but the one that fits the context best is also greatly reinforced by identical wording and grammatical construction of the same phrase in Genesis 4:7. Speaking of the power of sin in human lives, the writer describes sin as "crouching at your door." The next sentence is identical in Hebrew language construction to our phrase in 3:16: "It desires to have you, but you must master it." In Genesis 3, the woman's desire is contrasted with a man's designated rule; in Genesis 4, sin's desire is contrasted with the necessity of man's mastering or ruling it. The passage seems to suggest that it is a woman's tendency to desire to take the leadership role.[1]

In essence, she will desire that the man be something he can never be. She will want him to fulfill her, complete her, and be united with her in ways that no one will experience on this side of Eden. Because of our inherent sin nature and the curses and judgments of Genesis 3, the man will never be able to be what he was supposed to be for her in God's original design. She will always want more from him or dream that she can find more elsewhere. He will begin to resent her demands, and the struggle for power and control continues.

God judged the woman's ability to fulfill the creation mandate (to fill the earth, she would suffer pain in childbearing) and her relationship to her husband. Instead of enjoying intimacy and delight, men and women, as a result of the fall, will fight for power. The man will struggle with issues of control and manipulation. He will use her desire for him and exploit it for his benefit.

This dynamic is universal, and it is a reflection of God's mercy because He uses it to call both men and women back to Himself. But let's focus on the posture men normally have toward human relationships, especially toward women. We are fundamentally drawn to power and control and are continually tempted to use others to advance our own ideals and agendas. This can happen passively (we withdraw from competing with others altogether and learn to express anger, fear, or power through isolating ourselves and punishing others with our silence), or actively (we seek to one-up those around us by having more money, influence, ability, success, personality, or sheer willpower and find affirmation in our superiority). This takes place over the entire network of human relationships, but it is particularly present in the relationships between men and women.

When Good Guys Go Bad

Larry Crabb, noted author and psychologist, argues that men generally relate to others in one of two fundamental patterns. Some guys are ruled by a passion for neediness and others by a passion for tough-ness.[2] Men ruled by neediness require something from the people and relationships in their lives. Men ruled by toughness go the opposite extreme and pretend not to need anyone at all. Though the smaller of the two groups, men ruled by the passion of toughness fit the traditional image of tough-guy masculinity. They feel they can handle things best by themselves and prefer to remain distant and aloof. John Wayne, Clint Eastwood, and Arnold Schwarzenegger are their heroes.

Both kinds of men are controlling and manipulative. Both kinds of men fit the patterns of Genesis 3. And both kinds of men need the redemption of Jesus to reorient themselves to others.

Because the media and culture have ruthlessly dismantled the tough-guy image of masculinity (according to current cultural understandings, real men these days are supposed to be tender, sensitive, and caring), and because, according to Crabb's definitions, the needy group forms a larger percentage of men, we'll spend our time in this chapter looking at the pattern of neediness that Crabb describes.

All men are needy in one sense or another. The tough guy who doesn't need anyone is just as needy as anyone else; his lack just looks far different. Our needs, though, are hardwired into us. That is part of what it means to be created and human. We need others, need God, and need certain things for a fulfilling life. But what Crabb identifies as the passion of neediness is something deeper than this built-in dependence. Men who are needy in this way demand something from their relationships. Something within them is broken or missing, and they insist that others meet that need. They require those around them to treat them or respond to them in a certain way. These men manipulate others (consciously or not) in order to get the desired response from them. They may appear incredibly masculine, or come across as having it all together, but their aim is the same regardless of their appearance: They want to get something from another person.

I hate the word *needy*. It is the opposite of what I think of when I think of true masculinity. But it describes more of us than we'd care to admit. Crabb used an example to illustrate this sort of neediness that hit me right between the eyes. A woman describing her relationship with her husband was sharing why she always felt she had to come through for him:

> It could be a sigh when he walks in the door or a comment about traffic on the way home. Sometimes he tells me how tired he feels. It could be anything. But it's always about him, about something that's wrong, like I'm supposed to do something. Even when he asks about me, I feel set up to ask about him. If he helps with dinner, I get the look that tells me I'm supposed to tell him how wonderful he is.
>
> And if I do something special for him, even something little, like a really affectionate greeting, he's too appreciative. It makes me feel like he really needed it. That I better keep on

giving it to him, or he'll be really hurt. Sometimes when he's extra thoughtful, I think he's telling me I better be available for sex, but lots of times it's not that. I don't know how else to put it—everything he does makes me feel that I'm supposed to come through for him.[3]

When I read this, I had to laugh out loud. I had always considered myself a tough guy. I played football and rugby, love all the traditional masculine pursuits (success, girls, sports, and BBQ), and have zero fashion sense. I am big and bald and should have been a bouncer. The last word I would have used to describe myself was *needy*. Needy guys love emo, the food network, and all that is metrosexual. But when I read this section in Crabb's book, particularly reading what this woman said about her husband, I began to see otherwise. My wife has used the same language to describe me.

I want approval. I crave it. For some reason, I don't feel as if I have enough, so I seek it out from others. I use them, so to speak, to fill that need. I perform; they applaud. I sacrifice or serve; they notice and approve. I listen to others but want them to notice what a great listener I am.

I realized that power and control look different from what I had thought. Sure, I had been around guys who drank too much beer, insulted the women around them, and generally didn't care what anyone thought about them. Their embodiment of Genesis 3 was obvious. They were domineering and destructive. They were angry and easily set off. What I didn't realize, however, was the depth and breadth of masculine depravity. It did not occur to me that I was just as full of self and exploitation as they were.

Power Trip

This is the point of this chapter: Power struggles come in all shapes and sizes. Some are quite obvious, like two boxers pounding each other while going the distance in a heavyweight fight. But others are hidden behind a smooth veneer of niceness and civility. They may be more like the Cold War: a long series of small and subtle battles that add up over time.

The conflicts between men and women go back to Adam and Eve. She ate, and he didn't lift a finger to stop her. He ate and then blamed her for causing him to disobey. We see how insane it looks for them, but what we don't see is how much it drives us. Added to that is the reality that wives know their husbands well enough to know their weakness and failures. As much as we pretend otherwise, we really are fragile creatures. Our wives can help or hurt us more than anyone else. Many men secretly fear their wives for precisely this reason. We fear being exposed as a failure as a man, husband, or dad. One of the reasons men love ruling or dominating their wives is that their wives are most capable of hurting them.

The drive to rule over others takes so many forms, I fear we too easily buy the lie that says it only happens when men emotionally, physically, or sexually abuse their wives, demand they submit without respecting their opinions, or are threatened by others' success or income. Even the nicest of us has this darkness within him. I do want my wife to cater to me. I want my friends and coworkers to meet my needs. The holes in my heart and the wounds I've sustained push me to achieve and perform in the hope that approval and affirmation will someday bring healing. You wouldn't look at me and see a guy abusing power and control, but I do it nevertheless.

We can control our lives and the lives of others using money, influence, charm, physical strength, or anything else at our disposal. For some of us, money is the perfect means by which we can hide our neediness and show strength and power. For others of us, it's the kind of sex we like. For others, it's the way we treat people we perceive to be beneath us. And still others push their children to perform and excel as if to live their dreams through the lives of their kids. Power struggles exist anywhere men can be threatened—at home, at work, with friends, and with women.

We can also see now how our neediness as men and the power and control we desire to exert over others are related. When we are weak, broken, and needy, we desire, above all else, to escape and feel differently. When we encounter areas of weakness, we'll retreat to areas of strength. A guy can get beat up at home, only to love how work makes him feel. He can be disappointed in his sex life, only to crave the raunchy encounters he has over the Internet. Men want to feel like men. And, in our normal and sinful state, that requires looking and feeling strong and powerful. Because we are needy deep in the core of our hearts, we yearn to find an escape where we can be strong. We learn a crucial lesson early on: If you are not strong, fake it.

That is why competition defines us. We need to know whether we measure up. We compete using salaries, cars, houses, wives, kids, religious and civic activities, stories, sports, you name it. Men are continually trying to one-up each other in order to look strong. Some men end up withdrawing from competition altogether because it leaves them frustrated and insecure. Others of us just keep trying to find our way, hoping we come across people less well off than we are so we can feel better about ourselves.

Somewhere deep within his soul, every man struggles to feel adequate. Manhood is made, not born. All through a man's life, he will try to define himself. In junior high or high school, he might try sports or academics. In college, some guys party harder than everyone else, as if that will establish their sense of manhood. In the work world, a man may think that position, power, and income will validate him. Some men report no such struggle; they have covered their worry with a thick blanket of success (business, ministry, financial, social). Most men, however, would admit to some uncertainty about their own ability to achieve something of real value.

The tendency of men in a fallen world is to try to escape the judgment of Genesis 3—that life will not work apart from God. We strive toward precisely the opposite conclusion—that we can make life work on our own terms, in our own strength. Crabb remarks, "I wonder if the central passion that rules our culture today is the passion to make life work."[4] This is why money, position, and possessions are so attractive to us men: They offer a certain (though ultimately illusory) amount of power and control. We spend years trying to tame the untamable frustration and difficulty inherent to life in a fallen world. All men long for Eden in ways that they barely understand.

Running from Weakness to Strength

Pornography is the perfect expression of masculine neediness and the desire to have power and control. It is the most perverted twist on the desire we all have to be naked and unashamed.

I can sit, without any of the demands of commitment, intimacy, or real human contact, and indulge my needs by searching through images of women designed to suit my appetites. If I like this kind of woman, I can go there and control her; or if I like another kind, I go somewhere else. In a sense, I make demands of these women. They must turn me on by fitting into my preferences and desires. I care nothing for them, for their identity as image bearers and their worth as coequals. What they are like in real life doesn't matter to me. For the sake of my need, they play a role in my fantasy and present themselves as available for me, anytime and anyplace. I am in complete control of these women, and they exist to alter my mood, soothe past hurts, and make me feel like a real man. There is no greater example of Genesis 3 than the implicit demands and judgments I make upon these women, with my pleasure and satisfaction as my sole concerns. Their welfare is secondary to my need.[5]

Porn allows men to be consumers, not lovers. It presupposes that a woman is a product to be used and consumed by someone who has no love, connection, and respect for her, someone who just uses her sexuality for a moment of satisfaction. But a woman is a human being, not a product or object. She bears God's image. When we treat her as an object to be sold and consumed, we not only strip her of her humanity but also strip and rob us of ours.

Many of us might be tempted to rationalize pornography by saying, "It's not hurting anyone else," or "It's not a big deal; it's just harmless fun." But that misses the deeper issue. Porn at its core is an assault on the femininity described in Genesis 1—women are equal to men, they are God's image bearers, and they are His precious and sacred creations. They are meant to be honored and respected, but instead they become objects to be mass-produced.

The result? We have a generation of women who starve themselves, binge and purge, or compulsively exercise to live up to our airbrushed ideals. Real-life women can't compete with porn stars and the images on magazines, so they give up or try to measure up. This goes way beyond masculine voyeuristic tendencies; it strikes at the heart of femininity itself.

And that's why men love it. Women exist for us (*As it should be,* many of us think). What we may think of as harmless manly fun is really about much more than looking at images on the TV or computer screen. It is about turning the masculine soul toward its worst impulses. It robs women and men of their humanity.[6]

This is the natural temptation of the masculine heart under sin: to run from weakness into strength in order to make life work for our benefit. To accomplish this, we grasp at anything that gives us power and control over the world around us. This dynamic is most clearly expressed in the relationships between men and women, but it is also found most everywhere else. Once men are confronted with the reality that they can't make life work—that they will always feel inadequate and not manly enough—they will work all the more to define themselves as men.

As we have pointed out, this is God's mercy. But one thing must be understood. The instructions of Jesus and the rest of the New Testament are designed to reverse this sinful tendency and help us reorient ourselves toward what God intended for men and women in Genesis 1–2.[7]

Chapter 12

THE FIRST AND THE LAST

I didn't marry you because you were perfect or because I always loved you. I married you because you gave me a promise. That promise made up for your faults. And the promise I gave you made up for mine. Two imperfect people got married and it was the promise that made the marriage. And when our children were growing up, it wasn't a house protecting them; and it wasn't our love protecting them—it was that promise.

THORNTON WILDER

We've arrived at one of the most abused and misunderstood passages in the entire New Testament:

21 Submit to one another out of reverence for Christ.

22 Wives, submit to your husbands as to the Lord. 23 For the husband is head of the wife as Christ is the head of the church, his body, of which he is the Savior. 24 Now as the church submits to Christ, so also wives should submit to their husbands in everything.

25 Husbands, love your wives, just as Christ loved the church

and gave himself up for her [26] to make her holy, cleansing her
by the washing with water through the word, [27] and to present
her to himself as a radiant church, without stain or wrinkle or
any other blemish, but holy and blameless. [28] In this same way,
husbands ought to love their wives as their own bodies. He
who loves his wife loves himself. [29] After all, no one ever hated
his own body, but he feeds and cares for it, just as Christ does
the church— [30] for we are all members of his body. [31] "For
this reason a man will leave his father and mother and be
united to his wife, and the two will become one flesh." [32] This
is a profound mystery—but I am talking about Christ and the
church. [33] However, each one of you also must love his wife
as he loves himself, and the wife must respect her husband
(Ephesians 5:21-33).

Much harm has been done because of the way this passage is usually
interpreted. It has often been used as another expression of masculine
power and control. But this was not Paul's intent. In fact, it was quite
the reverse.

Every New Testament teaching regarding the way men and women
(or husbands and wives) relate now, as disciples of Jesus, must be seen
in light of the judgments of Genesis 3. There, as you remember, God
judged the relationships between men and women so that instead of
being characterized by harmony, trust, and delight, they were now, at
their core, struggles for power. We looked at this dynamic in the last
chapter. What is so important to remember, however, is that the work
of Jesus is now seeking to reverse those curses and judgments and
bring humanity and all creation back into alignment with God's purposes (though that work won't be fully completed until Jesus returns).

This passage of Ephesians teaches us to reverse and reorient our
natural inclinations toward one another under the fall, because of what
Christ has done and is doing. This passage is reversing the curse, not
reinforcing it. If we interpret Paul's words here as another expression of
the power struggle between men and women, we miss his message
entirely.

Under Jesus, we are to live differently. That is Paul's point in verse 22. We, as disciples of Jesus, now submit to one another. The word *submit* here means to voluntarily place yourself under another person.

In other words (and this is expressed in many other New Testament passages, such as Philippians 2), to submit means to place something with great purpose and direction under something else. I submit myself to the traffic laws of the United States when I set aside my own convenience (I would love to drive 100 miles an hour and run every red light) and follow the laws out of concern for the welfare of others. My submission is voluntary (I don't have to follow traffic laws) and purposeful (I recognize that my submission to these laws protects others and myself). When I do this, I have submitted myself to something else.

Paul is saying that as disciples of Jesus (notice he hasn't said a thing about men and women at this point), we place others' well-being ahead of our own. We do this out of reverence for Christ, meaning that the way we treat other people is a reflection of how we feel about God. In the broad sweep of the New Testament, all believers are to submit to authority—everyone who is under government, believers within a local church, wives, children, servants or employees, and husbands. All are to possess a spirit of submission; this is not something to which only women were called.[1]

To submit to one another, then, means to serve others instead of always looking out for our own interests or how we can get ahead. We place ourselves voluntarily under other people in order to serve them and place their well-being ahead of our own. Instead of serving ourselves, we are placing others ahead of ourselves.

Most English Bibles do something very detrimental with this passage. After verse 21, my NIV Bible has a paragraph break and a section title (in this case, "Wives and Husbands"), which seem to separate verses 22-33 completely from verse 21. But this is not remotely the case in the original language.

Verses 21 through 33 were written to present one unit of thought. Paul introduced the concept of all believers submitting to one another and then gave it a specific application regarding husbands and wives. If you examine verse 22 in the original language, you will see that it is missing a verb. It can be translated, "the wives to their own husbands as to the Lord." The verb *submit* in verse 21 carries over into verse 22, which is a specific example or application of the general concept Paul introduced in verse 21.

In other words, verses 21 and 22 are linked grammatically and can be loosely translated like this: "Submit to one another out of reverence for Christ—[for example,] wives to your husbands as to the Lord." The verb in verse 22 comes from verse 21, which means you cannot separate them. We have often heard the call for wives to submit to their husbands, but this is in the context of all disciples of Jesus submitting themselves to each other. Both verses have to be together to make complete sense of Paul's thought. Verse 22 can only be understood in light of verse 21.[2]

Paul is saying this: The prevailing way disciples are to operate is to place their well-being under that of another: Wives (as a specific application of the general principle), place the well-being of your husbands ahead of your own.

To Lead Is to Die

Verse 23 explains why a wife is to do this: "For the husband is the head of the wife as Christ is the head of the church, his body, of which he is the Savior." There is much debate about what *head* means, but no matter how you understand it, the husband's headship over the wife is inextricably linked to Christ's headship of the church.[3] But notice that Christ's headship over the church is linked to His sacrifice for her: "just as Christ loved the church and gave himself up for her."

Jesus gave up His life for the church, and His headship over the church comes from this sacrifice. This means, at the very least, that the husband is the head servant or sacrificer in the marriage. To be the head in this respect means to give oneself away for the good of another. Headship in the New Testament is always taught in the context of sacrifice and service, and never in power and control.[4] Jesus had the best interests of people in mind, and this is to be the posture of loving husbands (and boyfriends and fiancés) as well.

This has nothing to do with domination, subjugation, or exploitation of women. Notice that even the amount of instruction is weighted toward explaining the husband's obligations toward his wife. If Jesus is the pattern of headship, we can safely assume that husbands are to take the lead in service and sacrifice in the family.

This entire passage of Paul's letter to the Ephesians was a radical departure from the social norms of his day. Social custom and Roman law made men the absolute rulers of their households. Often the biblical commands addressed to husbands, fathers, and masters were all made to the same person. This was the structural norm of most households. Women were assumed to be inferior to men and thus made to be ruled by them.

Paul challenges this old order and turns it upside down by insisting that a believing husband love his wife—which had very little to do with marriage in that culture—and to love her as Christ loved the church. In the new order, under Jesus, the husband and wife are first of all brother and sister in Christ, and this radically alters their perspective. She is no longer just a member of his household; they are members of Christ's body.

The concepts of submission (placing oneself under), service, and sacrifice were radical to first-century men, and I think they are still relatively foreign to most men today. For many of us, due to our natural, sinful inclination toward power and control, we like to be served rather than to serve, to have someone look out for us instead of reorienting our lives for the benefit of another. This is how these passages reverse the judgments and curses of Genesis 3. Men, instead of ruling over wives and women, are now to love and sacrifice for them. Women, instead of desiring to control or change their husbands to be what they want, are now free to submit to them by trustingly placing their husbands' well-being ahead of their own.[5] Paul's instructions are not reinforcing the curse, but breaking it. He's showing how men can kill off the me-first mentality that infects too many of us.

Men, think about the implications of this. Jesus is our example.[6] He took time for Himself and fulfilled the Father's call for Him, but He did so in a way that brought life, goodness, and truth to those around Him. That is why we find it so noble when a man goes without food when there isn't enough food for his family or when a man works three jobs so his family can have a roof over their heads. Every culture on the planet recognizes that men are to do this. The goal of the head is to serve those around him. Whatever *head* means, it is tied to the sacrifice of Jesus.[7]

> You know that those who are regarded as rulers of the Gentiles lord it over them, and their high officials exercise authority over them. Not so with you. Instead, whoever wants to become great among you must be your servant, and whoever wants to be first must be slave of all. For even the Son of Man did not come to be served, but to serve, and to give his life as a ransom for many (Mark 10:42-45).

Easier said than done, right? But how many wives would joyfully and willfully submit to husbands who treated them that way?

Husbands are to follow the example of Christ and to grow as servants of those who are closest to them. We are to live lives of such loving devotion that we would lay down our lives for our wives and families. This sacrifice doesn't include ignoring needs, wishes, and desires. Our service has to be balanced, of course, as was Jesus'. He sometimes withdrew from the crowds, prayed alone, or stopped for rest and refreshment. We too should serve and lead our families without ceasing to be the men we are called to be.

My Love Is Self-Seeking

We have seen that God loves props—physical pictures of spiritual reality.

Paul talks about the relationship between wife and husband (and even quotes Genesis 2 to make his point) and then mentions a "profound mystery" that he is exploring. We naturally think the mystery is marriage. But Paul insists that it is the relationship between Christ and the church.[8] This means that the relationship between a husband and wife ought to be a picture of the relationship between Jesus and His church.

This has staggering implications for us men. It means that the purposes of marriage are larger than just marriage. Yes, it is not good to be alone, and procreation and sexuality are part of what it means to be human. But that isn't the sole point of the marriage covenant. The point of marriage isn't just to have a good marriage; it is far deeper than that. In some mysterious way, a godly marriage points to the message of God's kingdom in Jesus: Married couples are to have such love and devotion that a husband will lay down his life for his wife and a wife will joyfully place the well-being of her husband ahead of her own. They are to serve each other in such a way that the broken world around them will see Christ in them.

Christian marriages are to be living examples of the message of Jesus. He desires to use your marriage to draw others to Him as they see the way you and your wife sacrifice for each other. Marriage demonstrates a spiritual reality: It is a picture God has created in all of its wonder, beauty, and struggle, that the way two people love each other might be a witness to a hurting world.

This whole discussion became very personal for me during a particular counseling session when I was talking about all that was wrong with my wife (after months of talking about all that was wrong with me). Though there are many abuses in the Christian counseling movement, I benefited greatly from my time in therapy. One conversation with my counselor, Ted, brought this Ephesians discussion home in a profound way.

> Ted: "What do you wish your wife would do differently? Or what do you wish she would do that she is not doing?"
>
> Me: "That's easy." (I then went on to list a few things I would love to see her change.)

Ted: "Now, what would your marriage look like if you gave up your right to those things and loved her anyway?"

Me (after a long period of silence...): "Oh man—that's a great point."

That is the essence of masculine headship: giving up my right to having my marriage my way and loving my wife as she is. When Paul talks about love in 1 Corinthians 13, he mentions that "love is not self-seeking." For most of my life, my love has been the opposite: self-seeking. I loved in order to be loved and withheld love to punish people for not loving me well. The Scriptures call husbands (and dads, fathers, boyfriends, coworkers, and friends) to cease loving people to meet their own needs and actually endeavor to meet others' needs.

My marriage has experienced a radical shift in direction since I learned this. For years I have been trying to get my wife to love me in the ways I want (and think I need). But real, masculine, biblical love gives itself away without strings attached. Jesus showed us that this is what God's love is like.

That is why biblical marriage is like the gospel. For marriage to work, I have to understand that my commitment to keep my promise and to do right must take precedence over what I prefer.

Weaker Vessels?

People often debate about how men and women should relate to one another. I think much of this discussion misses the point. I refuse to accept a dichotomy between biblical headship and the Bible's teaching about the absolute, fundamental, and unalterable equality of women. Whether we like it or not, the Bible teaches both. My point here is that the New Testament calls husbands to move away from power and control and to serve and lead their wives as equals.

Men can hold various positions on this issue and still miss the force of what Paul (and the rest of the New Testament) is calling us to. We are called to abandon self-interest, self-centeredness, and self-absorption, not only as disciples of Jesus but also as men and husbands. Our theological positions are irrelevant if we miss this point. Paul is calling us away from the selfishness that characterizes the hearts of men.

Because my wife is my equal, I am head over her in a very specific and careful way. I treat her with dignity and respect because she is my equal not because she is needy or weak. Paul uses the example of the way men treat their own bodies to convey this point.

Peter echoes this point as he calls men to live considerately with their wives (1 Peter 3:7). This means that as I live with my wife, I consider a wealth of knowledge about her needs and concerns. To love my wife this way means that I treat her with care because she is a woman and not a man. I don't demean her for what she likes or finds interesting. I accept that she is different from me, and I learn to appreciate those differences. She is equal but not the same, so Paul, Peter, and others call men to treat women and wives differently than we treat other men. We treat them uniquely because they are unique.

Often we don't discover these deep differences until well into marriage. Once the honeymoon is over and the marriage settles into predictable routine, the wounds that our wives have carried for years may start to seep out. We begin to see our wives' brokenness.

> The great surprise is that she is broken. Often her brokenness will remain hidden until she becomes engaged, or married, and then wham—it all comes out. Why is that? You'd think now that she is safe, now that she knows she's loved, her soul can quit pushing it all down. But that's just it—now that she *is* safe and loved, her soul can quit pushing it all down. Before she is pursued and wanted, she fears that she cannot be herself or no man will want her. Now that she is loved, her heart comes forth and with it the sorrow of her life.[9]

This is when headship is most needed, as well as our new understanding of courage (discussed in chapter 2)—embracing life, our wives, and our jobs as they are, not as we want them to be.

Self-Sacrifice

This kind of self-sacrifice, I believe, is hardwired into the heart of every man. It may take a million different forms, but we are at our masculine best when we become this kind of a man. John Eldredge observes that men have "forgotten the deep pleasure of spilling our life for another."[10] Stu Weber argues, "The kind of man who pleases God is a man of his word. One who stays and keeps promises. One who 'swears to his own hurt.' *One who stays.* That kind of man creates an atmosphere of stability in an ocean of insecurity...the heart of staying power is sacrifice—giving up one's self for the good of another."[11]

According to Jesus, the way to thrive and flourish is to help others thrive and flourish. In other words, the way to fulfill yourself is to spend yourself. Jesus Himself tried to get this lesson across to the disciples by washing their feet.[12] We will not be fulfilled as men, even Christian men, until we first learn that we were meant to spend our lives, gifts, strength, and resources on behalf of others.

But this is hard to believe. We live in a culture that constantly reinforces the idea that masculinity is measured by the size of our penises, bank accounts, biceps, houses, or egos. We are taught that strength is seizing the initiative, outdoing the other guy, and winning at competition. That is true to some degree, but it leaves unnourished that part of a man's heart that wants to sacrifice for others. Making ourselves sacrifice for others (physically or otherwise) is usually difficult, but after we do, we feel good. We feel alive. Something about self-sacrifice taps into the heart of every man. God designed us this way, and Jesus embodied it perfectly.

This transition isn't easy, natural, or quick. It only comes about as we grow to become like Jesus more and more. We must begin by emptying ourselves of all vestiges of what Paul calls "the old self" (Colossians 3:9). This is the work we do in partnership with Jesus, denying ourselves, taking up our realities and our commitments, and following Him. This means coming to God on His terms, not ours, without negotiation or compromise.

For most of us, this issue plays out most clearly in what we decide to do with all that we have been given. We must decide if it is all for our benefit alone or for the benefit of others. For many of us, our influence and incomes have led us to lives of indulgence and comfort. For others, they have led to service and sacrifice. Never has the temptation been stronger to use what we have been given (such as strength, personality, talent, money, trust, and fame) to promote ourselves. These days, success tests our character more than failure does. Rohr puts the dilemma well:

> The gift [whatever has been given to a man] here is given
> *for others*. The quest and the grail are not for power, prestige
> or private possession. It is always for the sake of the com-
> munity, for the common good. I wonder if we even understand
> this stage anymore. For too often our concern seems to be
> development of our retirement account, self-serving politics
> and developing our personal image. No civilization has ever
> survived unless the elders saw their duty to pass the gifts of
> Spirit on to young ones. Is it that we are selfish, or is it that
> we ourselves have never found the gift? I suspect it is largely
> the latter. I don't think most people are terribly selfish; they just
> don't *know*.[13]

The call to men transcends the call to husbands; the latter is but one expression of the former. The reason we have examined the relation-ship between husbands and wives is to show the ways in which God calls (and empowers) men to leave self-interest and power behind and to give themselves away. That is the core of the masculine nature under Jesus. We follow His example in that regard. Whether married or single, young or old, Republican or Democrat, rich or poor, the fulfill-ment of the masculine journey will stay beyond our reach until we see this clearly. Men were made to spend themselves on behalf of others.[14] On battlefields, in boardrooms, or around dinner tables, men are at their best when they are using their masculinity for the good of those around them.[15]

There is simply no other way to be a godly man. The only options are the kingdom of this world or the kingdom of God, the gospel of

Donald Trump (or Michael Jordan, or Brad Pitt) or the gospel of Jesus. We have to choose again and again what kind of life we'll lead. Do we exist for others or for self? Will we really claim the life that is truly life through dying to all the other ways we could live?

C.S. Lewis comments on the realities that Christian husbands (and all men in their relationships with women in general) face:

> Christian law has crowned him in the permanent relationship of marriage, bestowing—or should I say, inflicting?—a certain "headship" on him...The husband is the head of the wife just in so far as he is to her what Christ is to the church. He is to love her as Christ loved the church—read on—and give himself for her. This headship, then, is most fully embodied not in the husband we should all wish to be but in him whose marriage is most like a crucifixion; whose wife receives most and gives least, is most unworthy of him, is—in her own mere nature—least lovable. For the Church has no beauty but what the Bridegroom gives her; he does not find, but makes her lovely. The chrism of this terrible coronation is to be seen not in the joys of any man's marriage but in its sorrow, in the sickness and sufferings of a good wife or the faults of a bad one...
>
> The sternest feminist need not grudge my sex the crown offered to it either in the Pagan or the Christian mystery. For the one is of paper and the other is of thorns. The real danger is not that husbands may grasp the latter too eagerly; but that they will allow or compel their wives to usurp it.[16]

Chapter 13

FATHERHOOD, BIOLOGICAL OR OTHERWISE

Perhaps there is nothing in this world as powerful
to break selfishness as is the simple act of looking at
our own children. In our love for them we are given
a privileged avenue to feel as God feels—to burst in
unselfishness, in joy, in delight, and in the desire to let
another's life be more real and important than our own.

RONALD ROLHEISER

I write this chapter with a no small amount of hesitation. I am 36
years old, and I have two kids, Nathan (four) and Hannah (two).
Both of these facts indicate that I am neither wise nor knowledgeable
in the ways of fathering. I am only a beginner.[1]

But as a novice, I am learning a few things that I wish I had experienced in my own childhood. So I write to those who are dads,
someday might be dads, have dads, or are foster, adoptive, or spiritual
dads.[2] I am primarily writing to me (I'm not so foolish as to tell you how
to be a dad), but I hope you might also find some blessing and benefit.

The Difference a Dad Makes

The status of the father has greatly diminished in our society at increasing cost. I'll start out with the bad news that illustrates just how important a father's role is in the lives of his children.[3] Forgive me for all the statistics to come, but including them is (apart from our own experiences) the best way to illustrate the point. We can show the importance of fathers by looking at what happens when they are not there.[4]

- An estimated 24.7 million children (36.3 percent) live absent from their biological fathers. A 1997 Gallup Youth Survey found that 33 percent of U.S. teens live away from their father; 43 percent of urban teens live away from their father.

- Today, only about 50 percent of children will spend their entire childhood in a biological two-parent family.

- In 2000, 1.35 million births (33 percent of all births) occurred out of wedlock.

- Forty-three percent of first marriages dissolve within 15 years. About 60 percent of divorcing couples have children. Approximately 1 million children each year experience the divorce of their parents.

- More than 75 percent of American children are at risk because of paternal deprivation. Even in two-parent homes, fewer than 25 percent of young boys and girls enjoy an hour a day of relatively individualized contact with their fathers.

- Sixty-three percent of all youth suicides are from fatherless homes. Ninety percent of all homeless and runaway children are from fatherless homes. Eighty-five percent of all children that exhibit behavioral disorders come from fatherless homes. Eighty percent of rapists, 71 percent of high school dropouts, 75 percent of adolescent patients in chemical abuse centers, 70 percent of juveniles in state-operated institutions, and 85 percent of all youths in prison grew up in fatherless homes.

- Children who live absent from their biological fathers are, on average, at least two to three times (one study has it at five to ten times) more likely to be poor, to use drugs, to experience educational, health, emotional, and behavioral problems, to be victims of child abuse, and/or to engage in criminal behavior than their peers who live with their married, biological (or adoptive) parents.

- Children with involved, loving fathers are significantly more likely to do well in school, have healthy self-esteem, exhibit empathy and pro-social behavior, and avoid high-risk behaviors such as drug use, truancy, and criminal activity, compared to children who have uninvolved fathers.

Stephen Arterburn quotes a study in Switzerland on the effects of a father's spiritual leadership on his children. It concludes, "It is the religious practice of the father of the family that, above all, determines the future attendance at or absence from church of the children." Here are some findings from that study:

If both a father and mother go to church regularly, 33 percent of their children will follow in their footsteps, while 41 percent will become irregular attendees.

If a father attends irregularly while his wife goes regularly, only 3 percent of the couple's children will become consistent churchgoers, while 59 percent become irregular.

If a father is a regular at church but his wife either is sporadic in her attendance or doesn't go at all, the percentage of children who will become regular churchgoers actually goes up to 38 percent, while 44 percent will become irregular worshippers as adults.

These statistics confirm what has long been common sense and parental intuition, as well as what the Scriptures teach. The influence of a father cannot be overstated. It affects every area of the lives of their children. Simply growing up in two-parent home is no guarantor of physical, emotional, or spiritual maturity, but it goes a long way toward providing an environment where maturity can develop.

Fatherhood, Biological or Otherwise

I find the role of a dad to be quite daunting. I didn't study it in school or learn much about it in seminary. Obviously I have a dad and have watched other dads, but on the whole I don't really feel equipped to handle the responsibility well. I have a hard enough time managing my roles as husband, son, brother, friend, and pastor without adding the role of father to the mix. But everywhere we look we have a dearth of fathers. We have males creating more males, but fathers are in short supply and great demand. Many men who should now be training their boys to be men are not yet men themselves. I fit that description perfectly.

Add to that the pressure churches put on men to be the spiritual leaders of their homes. I don't doubt that we are to be that for our wives and kids, but I have severe reservations about how that is usually played out. Scripture teaches that both mothers and fathers have parts to play in passing on the faith to their children.[5] I don't see this as only the job of the man.

We also harm men when we communicate that spiritual leadership comprises only a daily devotional hour for the family, consisting of a Bible reading, a story, a game, a memory verse, a prayer, and related activities. I don't know about you, but I wither under that expectation. When I try to do stuff like this, I feel phony and dumb. It just doesn't come naturally to me. I know some men for whom spiritual leadership in their homes is second nature. I'm not one of them.

So I have searched for ways to genuinely and joyfully show my kids my faith in and love for Christ.[6]

Honor My Father?

How many men walk around saying, "I want to be just like my dad"?

Far too many of us carry around a wound from our dads. Maybe he wasn't there physically, or maybe he was there, but he was silent and detached. Or he could have been mean, angry, and aggressive. Perhaps he never blessed or affirmed you, or he was very critical of your mistakes. Maybe he never showed affection, or maybe he was abusive. Many call these wounds *father wounds* because dads can hurt their children in lots of ways. Rohr comments on the nature of the father wound:

> Dads don't have to love us as moms do. Mom's love is body-based from the womb and the breast. Mom's love is taken for granted, relied upon instinctively, which is why a foundational "mother wound" can be even more devastating. My experience is that father wounds are much more common. His love is not inherently and instinctively felt and drawn upon, like mother love. He must choose to love you. He must notice you among the many...Father love redeems, liberates and delights in totally different ways than Mom's love.[7]

To be healthy dads (and sons, brothers, husbands, and friends) ourselves, we must first come to peace with our own childhood. We must come to peace with our fathers. For most of us, that means grieving our relationships with our dads. Don't excuse it or cover it up; cry over it and acknowledge that you wish it were different and that you can't think of a way to make it better.

The Israelites were commanded to "honor your father and your mother, so that you may live long in the land the LORD your God is giving you" (Exodus 20:12). Paul reiterates this command:

> Children, obey your parents in the Lord, for this is right. "Honor your father and mother"—which is the first commandment with a promise—"that it may go well with you and that you may enjoy long life on the earth" (Ephesians 6:1-3).

Honoring our father and mother doesn't mean pretending they were perfect. They weren't. But it does mean recognizing their place in bringing us life. God used my mom and dad (however imperfect they were) to bring me into the world. I don't know how to figure it all out; there is great mystery here. But I know that refusing to forgive them and staying angry at them for what they did (or didn't do) is not the way of Jesus. We don't have to say they were perfect, but we must come to peace with how God brought us into existence. If that doesn't happen, we'll be angry and bitter people, and we'll pass that on to the generations coming behind us.

Nor does honoring mean allowing them to run our lives. Sometimes we must break away from their direct influence over us. Two biblical examples are marriage ("For this reason a man will leave his father and mother and be united to his wife" [Genesis 2:24]) and discipleship to Jesus ("Anyone who loves his father or mother more than me is not worthy of me" [Matthew 10:37]). Honoring our dads means simply recognizing and appreciating the unique role they played in bringing us into the world.[8] Notice these commands to honor our parents say nothing about whether or not they are honorable. They just show that we must make peace with them and their role in our lives, whatever it may be.

If we don't do the hard inner work to forgive them, we will hand this stuff to *our* kids, becoming ourselves the very thing we despise.[9] This is why honoring parents is so central to fatherhood; otherwise, we become the very people against whom we have been rebelling.

You and I were shaped by our families and bloodlines. To be whole and healthy dads ourselves we must sort through our family issues and the way they shaped us. If we do not, we will pass on things we may not even be aware of. We are all driven by stuff from our childhood, and we're not even aware of it. Things that happened to me when I was eight or nine years old are still affecting me almost 30 years later.

Anger. Lust. Fear. Worry. Exaggeration. Jealousy. Slander. Bitterness. Alcoholism. Greed.

These things all betray us as wounded, broken, and sinful people. The work of Jesus is much bigger than just forgiving us (though we are very thankful for that); it also brings freedom, truth, and grace to those broken parts of our lives. Salvation isn't just about life in heaven; it is also about life now.[10]

Not all of us have been given a great childhood. Some things may have been handed down for generations and could now rest on you. Abuse, infidelity, alcoholism, depression, and abandonment—these are examples of generational things that get passed down. We are not isolated creatures who simply find ourselves alive today; we are the products of the generations before us. This is why fatherhood demands that we make peace with our fathers. We must honor and forgive them.[11] That is the first and most important step.

When my son was born, I started seeing things in me that I had never seen before. I grew increasingly angry and volatile; I pouted when I didn't get my way. I didn't understand what was going on. It was almost as if having an infant in our house gave me permission to be childish myself.[12] As Nate grew into a toddler, he loved and preferred his mom. If he was happy, he wanted Mom. If he was sad, he wanted Mom. I was acceptable only when Mom wasn't around. I began to resent my little guy for not wanting to be around me.

I was in counseling at this time, exploring my own wounds. My parents divorced when I was nine—the result of an affair. Thankfully, my parents were mature enough to share custody of my brother and me, but I have come to see that even though I was loved, the whole thing was more traumatic than I had realized. I had spent the years since the divorce searching in every possible way for approval and validation. I fit Crabb's definition of a needy man to a T.

I remember one day yelling at Nate (he was probably one and a half at the time) because he was crying and wanted his mother. I don't remember what I said (although it had to be a very mature, thoughtful comment, I'm sure), but I was so frustrated with the whole dad thing that I just caved in and started yelling at Nate and my wife. As I sat on our couch, the thought hit me that I was looking for Nate to validate me as a dad! At some unconscious, broken level, I was seeing his preference for his mom as a commentary on my fitness as a father. The more he wanted his mom, the worse I felt as a dad. That's a lot to put on a kid.

Once I saw this, I began to work on this issue (and the ones behind it) so that I would assume my role as father to bless him and encourage him regardless of what I got out of it. Today, we have a wonderful relationship (and he totally digs me over his mom), which would never have come about if I hadn't done the hard inner work to come to peace with my family.

This is the kind of stuff we carry around. And this is the kind of stuff Jesus wants to deal with. How many dads try to live through their kids? Or how many fathers do you know who pressure their children to act a certain way because they think the kids' behavior is a reflection of the parents?

Spiritual Fathering

Beyond honoring our parents, the Scriptures also command fathers to pass the faith we have in Christ down to our children. Paul writes, "Fathers, do not exasperate your children; instead, bring them up in the training and instruction of the Lord" (Ephesians 6:4). In this Paul echoes Asaph:

> He [God] decreed statutes for Jacob and established the law in Israel, which he commanded our forefathers to teach their children, so the next generation would know them, even the children yet to be born, and they in turn would tell their children. Then they would put their trust in God and would not forget his deeds but would keep his commands (Psalm 78:5-7).

As I said before, I don't think that raising our children in the Christian faith is solely the father's job. But I do think he plays a unique role, as we saw from the Swiss study. The real issue is this: How do parents pass along the faith? Moses gave the following commands to Israel:

> Hear, O Israel: The LORD our God, the LORD is one. Love the LORD your God with all your heart and with all your soul and with all your strength. These commands that I give you today are to be upon your hearts. Impress them on your children. Talk about them when you sit at home and when you walk along the road, when you lie down and when you get up. Tie

them as symbols on your hands and bind them on your fore-
heads. Write them on the doorframes of your houses and on
your gates (Deuteronomy 6:4-9).

This has been a very helpful passage for me, for it establishes a pattern for handing down my faith to my kids. Again, I am still a rookie at
this, but in the hope that something here might be helpful, I'll press on.[13]
Let's look at each part of this passage.

> Hear, O Israel: The LORD our God, the LORD is one. Love the
> LORD your God with all your heart and with all your soul and
> with all your strength.

Jesus calls this the greatest commandment.[14] This is what God desires
from us above all else. So the goal of passing along my faith isn't to
get my children to look Christian, act Christian, and sound Christian.
My goal as a dad is to hope, pray, and work in such a way that they
might love Jesus above all else. I am not alone in this; God Himself
joins me in this endeavor. But obviously I have a huge part to play.
And this part is far more than just teaching my kids good manners,
polite prayers, and religious behavior.

I want my children to see that they are part of a huge, epic story that
God wants to involve us in. Do I show my kids that my relationship
with Jesus affects every area of my life in a deep and passionate way,
or do they see only good morals and a few prayers? We need to
be captured by the whole Christian story rather than just the "don't do
anything bad" parts. I want my kids to see me risk, dare, and live in
dependence on an all-encompassing and good God. I want them to
have a real faith and joy, not just the feeling of having to perform some
list of empty religious duties.

> These commands that I give you today are to be upon your
> hearts.

Notice that before we impress these commands on our kids, they
must first be upon our hearts. I can't pass along what I don't have.
This doesn't mean I have to be perfect (our kids will have to come to

peace with *us* someday, and that is normal), but it does mean that my faith should authentically play out in front of my kids.

What that means for me as a dad is this: I want my kids to see no duplicity in my life. The man I am at church is the man I want them to see at home. I don't pretend and put on a religious act (kids will sniff that out in a second), nor do I pretend to have it all together. I think this is very important. My children have seen me get mad at Mommy and apologize. My children have seen me get mad at them and apologize. They have seen me succeed and fail.[15] I want them to see their dad knows he is imperfect but nevertheless desires to love and serve Jesus more and more.

Our kids have to see us fail; how else will they learn? They have to see us apologize, or they will never admit fault. They must see that following Jesus takes work (it's not just stuff you believe; it's stuff you live because of the stuff you believe), but it is worth every ounce of effort and grace.

> Impress them on your children.

This surely includes surrounding our children with a church community. I want to expose them to worship music, service, and teaching from their earliest moments. But far too many of us abdicate our spiritual responsibilities as dads, expecting the church to do the work for us. The church only gets our kids an hour or so a week; that is not enough time to override what they see at home. The church should equip us to be godly fathers rather than do the fathering for us.

As I said before, I feel lame doing family devotions. But because my kids are little, my wife and I have committed to reading Bible stories to our kids right after dinner.[16] We don't leave the table until we do this. We try to talk about what they learned and about what Daddy is learning too.

Another part of passing our faith along to our kids seems to be allowing them room to grow and feel and express faith differently according to age, maturity, personality, and most of all, gender. We have seen that boys and girls develop their spirituality in unique ways.

Boys should glory in being boys and girls should glory in being girls. Their devotion to Jesus should play out differently. The distinction between boys and girls must be expanded, not blurred, so that it can be reinforced in many other areas. We once made too much of the differences between men and women, and women suffered. But now we have gone to the opposite extreme and seek to erase gender differences altogether.

I don't know what my daughter will be like, but my boy is fully boy. He is smelly and fascinated by smelly things; he loves to push, wrestle, demand, and win; he does dumb and dangerous things for no discernable reason; and he is fascinated by all variations of the word *poo*. My boy is also surrounded by women: his mom (who is at home with him all day), his sister, his babysitters, his preschool teachers (two teachers and one aide), and most of his teachers at church. I love that, but if we are not careful, my little guy can begin to be pushed (consciously or not) into being something other than what he is: a smelly, sweaty, big and big-hearted four-year-old boy. I have realized that part of my job as Dad is to make sure he is given permission to be who he is. Not only at home but also at church and school.

Boys must be allowed to be boys, or they will never become men. Yes, they need to learn manners and the correct ways to handle burps and passing gas (so does Dad, in this case), but they should never be shamed for being boys. They need to learn to love Jesus in a "boy" kind of way.[17] We can't spend all our time warning them about getting hurt or not being up to a challenge; they need to be encouraged and dared into adventure in all its manifold glory. I have heard John Eldredge comment that much of the thrill-seeking behavior of boys is a search for deeper experience, something that is spiritual in nature, even though they don't know how to put words to it.

Talk about them when you sit at home.

Out of my vast fathering experience (yeah, right), I'm convinced that what children need most in order to grow into healthy men and women is the affirmation of their father (or a father figure). The home should be a place of blessing and encouragement above all else. All of Jesus' recorded ministry and accomplishments came after His Father's blessing, not before.[18] Jesus was also affirmed again by His Father before He began His journey to Jerusalem to die.[19] The power of a father's blessing is also displayed throughout the Old Testament (Jacob and Esau's story is the most familiar).[20]

Blessing our children is different from building up their self-esteem. Blessing our kids tells them that they are loved (by God and us) more than they can possibly imagine, that that love will never disappear or fade, and that they are not the center of the universe.[21] Blessing means showing and telling them that they have a part to play in God's story, not just their own. Self-esteem makes self the center and object. Blessing makes God the center and object. Blessing invites kids to play their part in the work of God.

Lately, I have taken the blessing that Jesus received from His Father—"This is my son, whom I love; with him I am well pleased"—and started praying and saying that over my kids. I discipline with this blessing in mind, and I compliment and affirm them likewise. This becomes the framework for my stewardship of them. God entrusted them to me and called me to raise them to love Him, so I bless them as He does. I simply say out loud what God thinks of them already.

This changes, of course, as they grow older, and it becomes increasingly important. It is an almost universally observed truth that a community of men bestows masculinity on a boy; only men decide when a boy has become a man.[22] So as my boy grows older, he must see not only his dad affirming him as a man but also other men. Initiation rites for boys around the age of 13 are becoming much more common in the Christian community.[23]

If boys don't receive these blessings, they (and the men they become) will continue to seek affirmation from everything and everyone.

Women, money, sports, work—men will use all these as they try to fill the hole left by the lack of fatherly affirmation. Because a boy derives his masculine identity from his father, the way dads treat their sons has far-reaching and potentially devastating consequences. Many of us walk around wounded and looking to heal that wound because we never heard our dads say they were proud of us.

One other thing that (I hope) characterizes our home is that we closely monitor what our kids see and hear. We aren't sheltering prudes, but we recognize the power that images have over us. I have sat through many cartoons with my kids, for example, to try to figure out what subtle messages they are conveying. A couple of very popular ones never have adults in them. The stories are about kids trying to solve their own problems without anyone older and wiser helping them out. We have banned those cartoons from our home because we want our kids to learn the opposite truth: You are never by yourself. You can learn from others and lean on them when you need to. Maybe if we dads (and dad types) did a better job of watching stuff with our kids, we would get into all sorts of discussions about what life is really like.

I also want our kids to see that I love and treasure my wife. We make a big deal to them about our weekly date nights so that they will learn that working on my relationship with my wife is the best thing I can do for my kids. I want them to see us hug, kiss, flirt, compliment each other, delight in each other, and fight with and apologize to each other. I want them to see that we fought to keep romance alive and worked hard at our relationship.

> ...and when you walk along the road, when you lie down and when you get up.

I had a friend named Doug who was great at bringing one or both of his boys with him everywhere he went. In fact, I cannot remember a time when I saw Doug without one of his boys by his side.

Doug embodied what Moses was talking about. As you go along in life—to work, to run errands, whatever—take your kids with you. Never go anywhere by yourself if you don't have to. My kids are just now old enough for me to start doing this. And, to be honest, I love it. Nate, Hannah, and I go out for breakfast at least three times a month; we drive a lot together—to preschool, the store, and church. I always try to take advantage of those times with them by asking about their day, what they think about things, and so on.

This isn't fancy stuff; it's just a matter of bringing our kids with us as we go about our lives and taking advantage of the unforced teaching moments that pop up. By seeing how you and I interact with the world "out there," our children begin to see that we, as disciples of Jesus, live in a world that doesn't revolve around us. We are part of a much larger story.[24]

Don't for a second buy the lie that says that quality time makes up for a lack of quantity time. The quality of time with our kids is directly related to how much time we spend with them in the first place. Both are equally important.[25]

> Tie them as symbols on your hands and bind them on your foreheads. Write them on the doorframes of your houses and on your gates.

Moses is speaking here of reminders, things that bring to mind how good God is and how we should live in response. For me, that looks like making memories with my kids. I want them to experience certain regular traditions that they can be shaped around. We do Christmas a certain way, Easter a certain way, birthdays a certain way, anniversaries a certain way, vacations a certain way. By taking advantage of the natural rhythms and holidays of the year, we naturally create regular memories and spiritual moments with our kids.

Being a good father is more about lifestyle than about regular scheduled spiritual events. We know that we raise our own biographers, so we capture every moment we can and hope that our love for our kids covers the mistakes we make along the way.

DISSIDENT JESUS

Once you domesticate Jesus, he isn't there anymore.
The domestic Jesus may be an interesting fellow, a good
friend, a loyal companion, a helpful business associate, a
guarantor of the justice of your wars. But one thing he
is certainly not: the Jesus of the New Testament. Once
Jesus comforts your agenda, he's not Jesus anymore.

ANDREW GREELEY

The Man Jesus

When most of us think of Jesus of Nazareth, we think in terms like
Savior, Lord, God, and *King.* Maybe, if we have spent enough time in
the Bible, we have a semi-grasp on the idea that He was fully human
and experienced all that we do except for sin. But I think very few of
us look to Jesus as an example of what it means to be a *man.* We
don't think of Jesus as masculine; we either think of Him as nice and
soft (like Mr. Rogers) or we don't think of Him as masculine at all.

As I've come to know Jesus, not as a religious figure but as a man who
walked the earth announcing and demonstrating the invasion of God's
kingdom into the kingdoms of the world, different words now come

to mind: *revolutionary, subversive, angry, passionate, dissident, alive.*[1] They haven't replaced the other words and titles, but they add meat and bones to often dry and abstract theological concepts.

One of the reasons men avoid the church is that Jesus isn't always presented as He really was. Most of the time we are not true to the Gospel accounts of Him; we've cleaned them up and made Jesus polite and always kind.

I was shocked when I began discovering that Jesus wasn't always nice. He grew impatient, used sarcasm, avoided questions, and forcefully confronted others. His life was characterized by conflict and antagonism.

He had conflict with the unseen powers of the world:

> Just then a man in their synagogue who was possessed by an evil spirit cried out, "What do you want with us, Jesus of Nazareth? Have you come to destroy us? I know who you are—the Holy One of God!" "Be quiet!" said Jesus sternly. "Come out of him!" The evil spirit shook the man violently and came out of him with a shriek (Mark 1:23-26).

> He also drove out many demons, but he would not let the demons speak because they knew who he was (Mark 1:34).

> So he traveled throughout Galilee, preaching in their synagogues and driving out demons (Mark 1:39).

> Whenever the evil spirits saw him, they fell down before him and cried out, "You are the Son of God." But he gave them strict orders not to tell who he was (Mark 3:11-12).

> He shouted at the top of his voice, "What do you want with me, Jesus, Son of the Most High God? Swear to God that you won't torture me!" For Jesus had said to him, "Come out of this man, you evil spirit!" (Mark 5:7-8)

Jesus had conflict with His family and neighbors:

When his family heard about this, they went to take charge of him, for they said, "He is out of his mind" (Mark 3:21).

"Isn't this the carpenter? Isn't this Mary's son and the brother of James, Joseph, Judas and Simon? Aren't his sisters here with us?" And they took offense at him. Jesus said to them, "Only in his hometown, among his relatives and in his own house is a prophet without honor." He could not do any miracles there, except lay his hands on a few sick people and heal them. And he was amazed at their lack of faith (Mark 6:3-6).

All the people in the synagogue [at Nazareth] were furious when they heard this. They got up, drove [Jesus] out of the town, and took him to the brow of the hill on which the town was built, in order to throw him down the cliff (Luke 4:28-29).

Jesus had conflict with His disciples:

"Why are you so afraid? Do you still have no faith?" (Mark 4:40).

"Are you so dull?" (Mark 7:18).

"Do you still not see or understand? Are your hearts hardened? Do you have eyes but fail to see, and ears but fail to hear?" (Mark 8:17-18).

But when Jesus turned and looked at his disciples, he rebuked Peter. "Get behind me, Satan!" he said. "You do not have in mind the things of God, but the things of men" (Mark 8:33).

Jesus had conflict with the religious leaders:

- About forgiving sins (Mark 2:1-12).

- About eating with sinners (Mark 2:15-17).

- About His religious practices (Mark 2:18-22; 7:1-13).

- About keeping the Sabbath (Mark 2:23–3:6).

- About His authority (Mark 11:27-33).

> Then the Pharisees went out and began to plot with the Herodians how they might kill Jesus (Mark 3:6).

> The chief priests and the teachers of the law heard this and began looking for a way to kill him, for they feared him (Mark 11:18).

> And the teachers of the law who came down from Jerusalem said, "He [Jesus] is possessed by [a demon]! By the prince of demons he is driving out demons" (Mark 3:22).

Jesus had conflicts with the political leaders:

> At that time some Pharisees came to Jesus and said to him, "Leave this place and go somewhere else. Herod wants to kill you." He replied, "Go tell that fox, 'I will drive out demons and heal people today and tomorrow, and on the third day I will reach my goal'" (Luke 13:31-32).[2]

Jesus was confrontive and critical. He used sarcasm, and He insulted the religious leaders of the day. He called them hypocrites, blind guides, whitewashed tombs, snakes, and a brood of vipers. Imagine that happening today! Jesus wasn't endlessly polite, patient, and available. The dissident Jesus brought conflict and division to the world. He fought and argued and didn't stand apart and aloof from human suffering, especially suffering that other people caused.

Of course Jesus was kind, loving, and compassionate also. But we already know those things about Him. We lose sight of the politically incorrect Jesus, the Jesus who traded barbs and one-liners with His opponents. The Jesus who talks about hell, money, and divorce. The last words that Jesus' contemporaries would have used of Him are often the first words people use today to describe him: boring, predictable, safe, comfortable, religious, nice, polite.[3]

I used to think the God of the Old Testament was wrathful, capricious, and somewhat arbitrary, and the God of the New Testament was full of love and grace. But a closer examination of the Bible reveals that God, as revealed through Jesus, is much more wrathful in the New Testament than in the Old. In the Old Testament, unlike in the ministry of Jesus, no one was consigned to hell.

We, like the second-century heretic Marcion or Thomas Jefferson in the eighteenth century, conveniently excise from the Bible those parts of it we don't like. We have especially done this with Jesus. In our well-intentioned efforts to preserve Him as Son of God, we have lost how completely wild Jesus was. We don't like apologizing for Jesus' actions or words, so we just sort of conveniently pretend they are not there.

The Jesus we see in the Bible is full of flesh-and-blood masculinity. How often is He presented to the church as what Paul Coughlin calls "The Bearded Lady"?[4] How often is Jesus presented as someone who helps us get our lives together (maybe that's why so many of our wives want us to go to church) or keep up nice religious appearances?

What does this picture of Jesus do with the sarcastic Jesus? Or the Jesus with a whip, overturning the business tables at the temple? Or the Jesus who destroys families?[5]

The way the church usually presents Jesus to men kills off the masculine spirit instead of making room for it. Of course, we are not saying that Jesus was like John Wayne, Clint Eastwood, or any other ultramasculine stereotype. Our point here is that Jesus models for us the full spectrum of masculine expression: anger and tears, strength and weakness, passion and prayer, toughness and compassion. When we see the full breadth of Jesus' humanity, we feel free to embrace masculinity as an expression of our love for Jesus rather than a replacement for it.

Following the Dissident Jesus

For all the church's preaching, teaching, activities, and worship, are men better off? Are they more invigorated and challenged because of their involvement with the church or less so? Where are the bold prophets? Do intensity and anger have their place in the Christian church?

As a man, I want glory, honor, adventure, and conflict. I deeply want my life to count, and I want to live for something bigger than me. Is this wrong? Can it be reconciled with the truly godly life? Am I allowed to follow my passions, feed my ambitions, and feel my desires, all while keeping my life aimed toward Jesus?

The false pictures of Jesus lead to false pictures of Christian masculinity. I want to see those pictures change for me and for others. Why, as a pastor, do I feel compelled to be nice and polite and always available for everyone? Why do I often worry more about being nice than being good? Why do I feel that being aggressive, assertive, or confrontational is wrong? None of these things were true of Jesus, but why, as a man, do I feel the need to embrace them now?

Take anger, for instance.[6] Jesus was angry quite often. Here's an example:

> Another time [Jesus] went into the synagogue, and a man with a shriveled hand was there. Some of them were looking for a reason to accuse Jesus, so they watched him closely to see if he would heal him on the Sabbath. Jesus said to the man with the shriveled hand, "Stand up in front of everyone." Then Jesus asked them, "Which is lawful on the Sabbath: to do good or to do evil, to save life or to kill?" But they remained silent. He looked around at them in anger and, deeply distressed at their stubborn hearts, said to the man, Stretch out your hand" (Mark 3:1-5).

Here Jesus picked a fight. He could have healed the man privately or at another time, but instead He has him stand up in front of everyone. The man didn't ask to be healed; Jesus went looking for conflict.[7] His opponents would not even answer the questions He put to them, so "he looked around at them in anger." The word here speaks of intense desire mixed with grief. It is circumstantial, which means that Jesus didn't walk around an angry person looking for a reason to vent. Rather, this specific circumstance provoked Jesus to anger.

Here's another example: "People were bringing little children to Jesus to have him touch them, but the disciples rebuked them. When Jesus saw this, he was indignant" (Mark 10:13-14).

This was another situation that made Jesus mad. He wasn't a perpetually mellow dude spouting off pious slogans; some things made Him angry. The same is true of God in the Old Testament, which includes more than 300 references to God's anger or wrath against injustice, evil, cruelty, and sin.

Of course, Jesus' anger is much different from ours.[8] I can trust Him to be righteously indignant much more than I can trust myself. But simply because my anger may threaten to burn out of control doesn't mean that I shouldn't be angry at all. Paul himself counsels the church in Ephesus, "'In your anger do not sin:' Do not let the sun go down while you are still angry."[9] So people other than Jesus can be angry and not sin.

In these two examples, Jesus' anger led Him to heal the man with the shriveled hand and to receive children. In both cases, His anger led to something good and powerful. For most men, however, anger leads to harsh words, rude gestures, sullen silence, or sometimes, to violence. We are in desperate need of biblical instruction on the issues of anger and conflict, but very rarely do we hear anything from the church beyond "Don't be angry," or "Three Steps to Avoiding Conflict." Men are not given the opportunity to learn from Jesus in this regard (or from Paul, Peter, Moses, or God Himself for that matter). The soft, cuddly Jesus presented by the church doesn't help us in our bumpy, conflict-filled world.

Our world is upside down, and that is why Jesus' teaching so often seems to be the reverse of our natural inclinations. Jesus got mad at things that mattered, things that were important. I get mad at dumb, small things, like sitting in traffic, waiting in line, or being overcharged. I get mad if my wife doesn't react in the manner I prefer or when my kids are, well, kids. Christians, on the whole, seem to be insecure, easily offended victims.

This is a far cry from how Jesus and His disciples (not to mention the early church) saw themselves. Jesus wasn't small, petty, or vindictive. Garret Keizer remarked that Jesus has "the zeal of an ego identified by something larger than itself."[10]

Maybe we get angry about small stuff because we don't care enough about the big things—the things that made God angry. Maybe we don't see our lives as big enough or important enough, so we fly off the handle at the smallest slight. Maybe we were made to be angry—and to be fueled by rage—in order to fight against the forces that threaten our families, societies, and children. Maybe we were made for more than avoiding trouble and gaining disposable income.

> The church tells men that they aren't supposed to be angry about anything. Although avoiding anger does limit our ability to do damage, it also limits our ability to do good. Anger, by itself, is neither good nor bad—anger's rightness depends on the direction we move with its power and energy. But we Christians don't believe that anger is a good power source. By shunning all expressions of anger, we reduce our ability to be forces for redemption. Anger can propel our indifferent hearts into redemptive action.[11]

Could it be that as men we were made to fight? We see this in Jesus. He warred against all kinds of things. Do we stand up for those around us who have no voice of their own? Do we fight against the lies and falsehoods of our cultures? Do we fight to see our children educated fairly and our sons and daughters raised in an environment that respects as well as challenges them?

We are not talking about malice, insult, or a lack of self-control. We need to root out and deal with these kinds of anger by God's grace. But does the Christian life have room for anger? I think the answer must be yes. Does the heart of a Christian man have room for passion, intensity, and conflict? Here too, the answer is yes. Paul confronted Peter to his face (see Galatians 2:11-14 for the rest of the story), and Paul and Barnabas argued over Mark (see Acts 15:36-40). Seeing

Jesus clearly means embracing a full-orbed masculinity. Anger isn't always sin, nor is conflict. Sometimes the people of God sin by *not* being angry and by not going to war against the harmful things in our culture.[12] In fact, if we are not offending somebody, we might not be living as Christ would have us live.

C.S. Lewis describes perfectly the effect the church has on men:

> All the time—such is the tragi-comedy of our situation—we continue to clamor for those very qualities we are rendering impossible. You can hardly open a periodical without coming across the statement that what our civilization needs is more "drive," or dynamism, or self-sacrifice, or "creativity." In a sort of ghastly simplicity we remove the organ and demand the function. We make men without chests and expect of them virtue and enterprise. We laugh at honor and are shocked to find traitors in our midst. We castrate and bid the geldings be fruitful.[13]

Early Christians were known for risk taking, power, aggression, and heroic sacrifice. This is what men want. But today, to be a good Christian is to be nice, inoffensive, humble, dependent, nurturing, and supportive. We have lost the dangerous nature of being Christians. Men get the message that we are flawed in the way we are made, but Jesus reminds us of just the opposite. To be a Christian man is to still be a man and to experience everything that entails. Jesus is God. But He was also a flesh-and-blood man. We have to see Him as both.

Men, we must learn to see in Jesus the perfect example of all that we have discussed in this book. Being moderate and polite isn't always a virtue. Some things are worth fighting for. We were made for battle. That is life in a fallen world. But the battles we choose are so often not aligned to God's purposes in this world. What would happen if men rose up against injustice, oppression, pornography, and abuse? How would our sons and daughters see Jesus in us if they saw us passionately engaged in the world around us in order to bring glory and honor to Jesus?

We need to embrace the entire spectrum of masculinity: tough to tender, warrior to lover, student to teacher, empire builder to family builder. Unless this happens, masculine energy can lead men into damaging violence or brooding autonomy. We need to be captured by the person and kingdom of Jesus, knowing we have an important part to play, here and now, in shaping the world we live in.

A BRIEF WORD
TO PASTORS

> If I profess with the loudest voice and clearest exposi-
> tion every portion of the truth of God except precisely
> that little point which the world and the devil are at the
> moment attacking, then I am not confessing Christ, how-
> ever boldly I may be professing Christ. Where the battle
> rages, there the loyalty of the soldier is tested.
>
> MARTIN LUTHER

Much has been made of men's declining interest in the church. Here are a few snapshots of this trend not referenced elsewhere in this book.[1]

- The typical American congregation draws an adult crowd that is 61 percent female, 39 percent male. This gender gap is true across all age categories.

- On any given weekend there are 13 million more adult women than men in America's churches.

- This weekend almost 25 percent of married, churchgoing women will worship without their husbands.

- Seventy to 80 percent of participants in midweek church activities are female.

- The majority of church employees are women (except for ordained clergy, who are overwhelmingly male).

- As many as 90 percent of the boys who are being raised in church will abandon it by their twentieth birthday. Many of them will never return.

- More than 90 percent of American men believe in God, and five out of six call themselves Christians. But only two out of six attend church on a given weekend. The average man accepts the reality of Jesus Christ but fails to see any value in gathering with a church community.

Stephen Arterburn, in *The Secrets Men Keep*, adds these statistics:

- Eighty-eight percent of men are often, always, or sometimes bored by the idea of church and church activities.

- Most men feel intimidated by their wives' spirituality; 68 percent said they don't measure up some of the time, often, or always.

Leon Podles sums up what many of us already know: "Despite constant feminist complaints about the patriarchal tendencies of Christianity, men are largely absent from the Christian churches of the modern Western world."[2]

Men have a more difficult time (than do women) finding significance and relevance in the local church. To be sure, an authentic relationship with Jesus is more than just weekly church attendance, but gathering with the community of believers is a significant indicator of such a relationship with Christ. So our concern about this trend is warranted.[3]

I can only speak from my experience, but I offer a few suggestions that I have found helpful in giving men permission to reconcile their masculinity with faith in Jesus:

Typical men's ministries feel like either women's ministries for men (they are structured the same, with the same kinds of events) or like a perpetual Super Bowl party with a superficial Christian veneer. We need to give men permission to be men regardless of what kind of men they are. That means being sensitive to the jocks as well as the artists, the construction workers as well as the musicians. If we are not careful, the church can subtly reinforce cultural masculine stereotypes that exclude some of our men.

I learned this lesson firsthand one year when several members of our male staff were talking about manly issues at our staff retreat. The subject of lust came up (surprisingly), and we began a discussion that just sort of assumed that every guy there struggled with it. In the midst of our conversation, one friend commented that he struggles with feeling unmanly because he doesn't struggle with the issue of lust. Our conversation changed at that point because we realized that more than one kind of man was sitting in the room, and we began to open up in ways that were significantly more beneficial.

Do we do justice to Jesus in His full humanity and masculinity? As we have seen, Jesus was a lot more passionate and intense than we usually give Him credit for. He was a revolutionary and a subversive insurrectionist. He was angry about the injustice of the religious and political oppression of His day. Perhaps we have softened Jesus up to the point where some guys just can't relate to "falling in love with Jesus," or having an "intimate and personal relationship" with Jesus. Maybe we need to develop more traditionally masculine expressions of worship and language. Dare we call men to fight against injustice and sinful structures of the world that hold so many men in bondage?

Do we call the men of church to more than family devotions, tithing, and church attendance? Are they captured by the broad and sweeping vision of God's kingdom as it advances around the world? Do men see their place in what God is doing, or do we merely teach them to be nice? I love N.T. Wright's invitation for us to participate in the gospel of Jesus:

Christian holiness is not (as people often imagine) a matter of denying something good. It is about growing up and grasping something even better. Made for spirituality, we wallow in introspection. Made for joy, we settle for pleasure. Made for justice, we clamor for vengeance. Made for relationship, we insist on our own way. Made for beauty, we are satisfied with sentiment. But new creation has already begun. The sun has begun to rise. Christians are called to leave behind, in the tomb of Jesus Christ, all that belongs to the brokenness and incompleteness of the present world. It is time, in the power of the Spirit, to take up our proper role, our fully human role as agents, heralds, and stewards of the new day that is dawning. That, quite simply, is what it means to be Christian: to follow Jesus Christ into the new world, God's new world, which he has thrown open before us.[4]

Our view of Jesus and His movement should be compelling and adventurous, risky and daring. Most men don't want more empty religion; they want to feel alive. Being a part of God's movement should have that effect, and if not, we need to honestly question whether we are understanding Jesus and His movement correctly.

How should we raise our boys in the church? Do they see Jesus as a buddy who teaches them to be good, or are they swept up into learning to find their place in *His* world? Do our boys have masculine role models who are showing them how to be men and worship and serve Jesus at the same time? Are we calling older men (as in 1 Timothy and Titus) to "father" the younger men of the church?

Are we showing men how to integrate their faith with their work? With their hobbies and pursuits? With their relationships with women? Do men see their faith as nothing more than religious obligation (which is piled on top of other obligations), or do they see that God is at work all around them—at their jobs, homes, schools—and that their job is simply to pay attention and join God where they find Him working already?

Do we talk about sex to our congregations? Are we honest about the struggles that our people (and we) have, and do we teach people how to deal with these in an honest and hopeful way?

As pastors, do we present ourselves as holy men or as men struggling to be holy? Are we honest about our own failures, struggles, account-ability, and need for forgiveness? Do we present ourselves as men to our men, or do we present ourselves as pastors, something more than a normal guy?

Are we, as leaders of God's church, working on our own wounds, hurts, and sin? Are we living the life we would want for our men? In Western church culture, we can easily live from one adrenaline high to another and live vicariously, watching God move in the lives of those we minister to, without seeing Him move powerfully in us. I found great benefit in reading Peter Scazzero's book *The Emotionally Healthy Church*. It contained some great advice about how to lead and create a church that is honest and healthy.

Introduction

Epigraph. Erwin Raphael McManus, Uprising: A Revolution of the Soul (Nashville, TN: Thomas Nelson, 2003), p. 5.

1. David Murrow, Why Men Hate Going to Church (Nashville, TN: Thomas Nelson, 2004).

Chapter 1—In the Image

Epigraph. Michael E. Wittmer, Heaven Is a Place on Earth: Why Everything You Do Matters to God (Grand Rapids, MI: Zondervan, 2004), p. 11.

1. Leon J. Podles, The Church Impotent: The Feminization of Christianity (Dallas, TX: Spence, 1999), p. 37.

2. See Luke 7:34, John 2:10; 1 Corinthians 10:23-26; 1 Timothy 4:3-4.

3. Tremper Longman III, How to Read Genesis (Downers Grove, IL: InterVarsity, 2005), p. 108.

4. See Job 38–41.

5. Nahum M. Sarna, Understanding Genesis: The World of the Bible in the Light of History (New York, NY: Schocken Books, 1966), p. 16.

6. Cornelius Plantinga Jr., Engaging God's World: A Christian Vision of Faith, Learning, and Living (Grand Rapids, MI: Eerdmans, 2002), pp. 52-53.

7. Richard Rohr with Joseph Martos, From Wild Man to Wise Man: Reflections on Male Spirituality (Cincinnati, OH: Saint Anthony Messenger, 2005), p. 7.

8. We'll look more closely at this point in a later chapter.

9. Quoted in Douglas Wilson, Future Men (Moscow, ID: Canon, 2001), pp. 17-18.

10. David Murrow, Why Men Hate Going to Church (Nashville, TN: Thomas Nelson, 2004), pp. 7-10,15-16.

11. Paul's statement in Galatians 3:28-29 that "there is neither…male nor female, for you are all one in Christ Jesus" does not mitigate this point. Paul is not arguing for some genderless ideal; he is making the revolutionary point that the distinctions often held to have religious significance (between Jew and Greek, for instance) are not valid in the kingdom of Jesus.

12. Stu Weber, Four Pillars of a Man's Heart: Bringing Strength into Balance (Sisters, OR: Multnomah, 1997), p. 39.

13. Dr. Larry Crabb, Men and Women: Enjoying the Difference (Grand Rapids, MI: Zondervan, 1991), pp. 132-49.

Chapter 2—On Being Strong and Courageous

Epigraph. John Eldredge, *The Way of the Wild Heart: A Map for the Masculine Journey* (Nashville TN: Thomas Nelson, 2006), p. 87.

1. Quoted in Douglas Wilson, *Future Men* (Moscow, ID: Canon, 2001), p. 120.

2. Gordon D. Fee, *Paul, the Spirit, and the People of God* (Peabody, MA: Hendrickson, 1996), pp. 144-50.

3. In contrast to Tim Riter, *Strong Enough to be a Man: Reclaiming God's Plan for Masculinity* (Kansas City, MO: Beacon Hill Press, 2005): "I'm convinced that strength defines maleness."

4. See John 5:19; 6:57; 10:30; 14:10.

5. Philippians 2:6-8

6. Hebrews 5:8

7. Erwin Raphael McManus, *Uprising: A Revolution of the Soul* (Nashville, TN: Thomas Nelson, 2003), p. 89.

8. C.S. Lewis, *The Silver Chair* (New York, NY: Harper Books, 1953), pp. 20-21.

Chapter 3—Naming the Animals

Epigraph. Charles Colson and Nancy Pearcey, *How Now Shall We Live?* (Wheaton, IL: Tyndale House, 1999), p. 392; quoted by John H. Walton, *NIV Application Commentary: Genesis* (Grand Rapids, MI: Zondervan, 2001), p. 192.

1. Cornelius Plantinga Jr., *Engaging God's World: A Christian Vision of Faith, Learning, and Living* (Grand Rapids, MI: Eerdmans, 2002), p. 15.

2. Michael E. Wittmer, *Heaven Is a Place on Earth: Why Everything You Do Matters to God* (Grand Rapids, MI: Zondervan, 2004), pp. 123-26.

3. David Bruce Hegeman, *Plowing in Hope: Toward a Biblical Theology of Culture* (Moscow, ID: Canon, 1999), p. 30. Much of this chapter benefited from this work.

4. Colossians 1:15-20

5. Colossians 3:17

6. Dr. Larry Crabb, with Don Hudson and Al Andrews, *The Silence of Adam: Becoming Men of Courage in a World of Chaos* (Grand Rapids, MI: Zondervan, 1995), p. 65.

7. Plantinga, *Engaging God's World*, p. 33.

8. Richard J. Mouw, *He Shines on All That's Fair: Culture and Common Grace* (Grand Rapids, MI: Eerdmans, 2001).

9. Wittmer, p. 132.

10. Richard Rohr with Joseph Martos, *From Wild Man to Wise Man: Reflections on Male Spirituality* (Cincinnati, OH: Saint Anthony Messenger Press, 2005), p. 62.

11. Rohr with Martos, *From Wild Man to Wise Man*, p. 63.

12. This is where a theology of art and creativity comes into being. See Hegeman, *Plowing in Hope*, pp. 113-22.

13. Plantinga, *Engaging God's World*, p. 121.

Chapter 4—Toil and Thorns

Epigraph. Cornelius Plantinga Jr., *Engaging God's World: A Christian Vision of Faith, Learning, and Living* (Grand Rapids, MI: Eerdmans, 2002), p. 15.

1. Derek Kidner, *Genesis: An Introduction and Commentary* (Downers Grove, IL: InterVarsity, 1967), p. 70.

2. Tremper Longman, *How to Read Genesis* (Downers Grove, IL: InterVarsity, 2005), p. 113.

3. Note what Paul says in Romans 8 about all of creation groaning. We are so connected to the environment that when we fell, so did it.

4. I am unsure of the origin of this quote.

5. Dr. Darryl Talley taught these two points in my Old Testament survey class at Talbot School of Theology.

6. For more on this point, see Richard Rohr with Joseph Martos, *From Wild Man to Wise Man: Reflections on Male Spirituality* (Cincinnati, OH: Saint Anthony Messenger, 2005), pp. 1-5.

7. See Romans 1:18-25.

8. Dr. Larry Crabb, with Don Hudson and Al Andrews, *The Silence of Adam: Becoming Men of Courage in a World of Chaos* (Grand Rapids, MI: Zondervan, 1995), p. 13.

9. Ecclesiastes 3:11

Chapter 5—Harps, Clouds, and Backhoes

Epigraph. J.I. Packer and Thomas Howard, *Christianity: The True Humanism.* Quoted by David Bruce Hegeman, *Plowing in Hope: Toward a Biblical Theology of Culture* (Moscow, ID: Canon, 1999), p. 65.

1. See Michael Wittmer, *Heaven Is a Place on Earth: Why Everything You Do Matters to God* (Grand Rapids, MI: Zondervan, 2004); Randy Alcorn, *Heaven* (Wheaton, IL: Tyndale House, 2004).

2. Believe me, I am incredibly grateful for forgiveness. I don't mean to minimize that aspect of the atonement; I just want to point out that Jesus accomplished more on the cross than individual forgiveness alone. For more, see Dallas Willard's *The Divine Conspiracy* or *The Nature of the Atonement: Four Views*, edited by James Beilby and Paul R. Eddy.

3. Genesis 12:1-3

4. Note the echo here from Exodus: "I will take you as my own people, and I will be your God" (Exodus 6:7).

5. Paul uses the same word in 2 Corinthians 5:17 and Galatians 6:15 to speak of people becoming a new creation. The Greek word used for *new* in Revelation 21:1-2 and 2 Peter 3:13 is not *neos* but *kainos*. This is significant. The word *neos* means new in time or origin (brand-new), while the world *kainos* means new in nature or quality. Thus the new heavens and new earth describes not the appearance of a universe totally other than the present one but a universe that has been divinely renewed and stands in real continuity with the present heaven and earth. (See David Bruce Hegeman, *Plowing in Hope: Toward a Biblical Theology of Culture* (Moscow, ID: Canon, 1999), p. 92.

6. Wittmer, *Heaven Is a Place on Earth*, p. 17.

7. Isaiah 60; 65:17-23; Matthew 5:5; Romans 8:21; 2 Peter 3:13; Revelation 21–22

8. 1 Corinthians 15:35-55; Philippians 3:21

9. Hegeman, *Plowing in Hope*, p. 88.

10. Rob Bell has said, "Do we go up or does God come down? God wants to be here with us. How many of the dominant American theologies are about us being afraid we will be left behind? The biblical story doesn't seem to be about people trying to escape this world but rather about God invading it."

11. N.T. Wright, *Simply Christian: Why Christianity Makes Sense* (New York, NY: HarperSanFrancisco, 2005), p. xi.

12. See also Revelation 5:10.

13. Revelation 14:13

Chapter 6—Naked and Unashamed

Epigraph. Peter Kreeft, *How to Win the Culture War: A Christian Battle Plan for a Society in Crisis* (Downers Grove, IL: InterVarsity Press, 2002), p. 95. Quoted by John Piper and Justin Taylor, *Sex and the Supremacy of Christ* (Wheaton, IL: Crossway Books), pp. 15-16.

1. 1 Corinthians 10:31

2. Cornelius Plantinga Jr., *Engaging God's World: A Christian Vision of Faith, Learning, and Living* (Grand Rapids, MI: Eerdmans, 2002), pp. 38-39.

3. For example, see Isaiah 62:4-5; Hosea 2:14-10; Ephesians 5:25-32.

4. Tommy Nelson holds this view. See his commentary on Song of Songs: *Book of Romance: What Solomon Says About Love, Sex and Intimacy* (New York, NY: Thomas Nelson, 1998).

5. Nelson, *Book of Romance*, p. 34.

6. Lauren Winner makes this point beautifully in her book, *Real Sex: The Naked Truth About Chastity* (Grand Rapids, MI: Brazos, 2005), p. 38.

7. Hebrews 4:15

8. Ronald Rolheiser, *The Holy Longing: The Search for a Christian Spirituality* (New York, NY: Doubleday, 1999), p. 196.

9. Read 1 Corinthians 6.

10. As an example, see Exodus 25.

Chapter 7—Not All Electric Shocks Are Bad

Epigraph. Philip Yancey, *Reaching for the Invisible God,* quoted in Paul Coughlin, *No More Christian Nice Guy: When Being Nice—Instead of Good—Hurts Men, Women, and Children* (Minneapolis, MN: Bethany House, 2005, pp. 109-10.

1. For those wondering about homosexuality and the push for society to recognize homosexual civil unions, I recommend *The Gay Gospel?* by Joe Dallas.

2. See Matthew 19:4-6; 1 Corinthians 6:16.

3. Ronald Rolheiser, *The Holy Longing: The Search for a Christian Spirituality* (New York, NY: Doubleday, 1999), p. 199.

4. Two great books on the subject are *Sex God: Exploring the Endless Connections Between Sexuality and Spirituality* by Rob Bell, and *Sex and the Supremacy of Christ* by John Piper and Justin Taylor.

5. Research conducted by the Barna Group has found no fundamental difference between the sexual lives of those within the church and those outside it. See www.barna.org for more information.

6. I don't mean to imply here that all sexual expression that goes on in the marriage relationship is good and holy. We know that not to be the case.

7. I am not making a distinction between sex and sexuality here. Expressions of sexuality run from holding hands to long romantic talks. These expressions are not reserved for marriage but do precede the kinds of expressions that are. For reasons that I hope will be apparent, I will not properly nuance the discussion to follow in this way. Rolheiser captures the distinction between sex and sexuality well: "Sexuality is an all-encompassing energy inside of us. It is the drive for love, communion, community, friendship, family, immortality, joy, delight, humor and self-transcendence...Genitality, having sex, is only one aspect of that larger reality of sexuality, albeit a very important one. Genitality is particularized, physical consummation, a certain privileged constellation of many of the energies that are contained within our wider erotic energies in one bodily encounter with another person which we commonly call making love." Rolheiser, *The Holy Longing,* pp. 194-95.

8. Song of Songs 2:7; 3:5; 8:4

Chapter 8—Victoria's Other Secret

Epigraph. Richard Rohr with Joseph Martos, *From Wild Man to Wise Man: Reflections on Male Spirituality* (Cincinnati, OH: Saint Anthony Messenger, 2005), p. 25.

1. For an excellent overview of the breadth and depth of human sin, I recommend Cornelius Plantiga Jr., *Not the Way It's Supposed to Be: A Breviary of Sin* (Grand Rapids, MI: Eerdmans, 1995).

2. This spiral of descent was adapted from a sermon by Rich Nathan, the pastor at Vineyard Columbus (Ohio).

3. For more on this point, see Psalm 115:8; 135:18. See also N.T. Wright, *Simply Christian: Why Christianity Makes Sense* (New York, NY: HarperSanFrancisco, 2006), p. 148.

4. R. Schuchardt, "Hugh Hefner's Hollow Victory," *Christianity Today*, Dec. 2003, p. 50.

5. "Therefore confess your sins to each other and pray for each other so that you may be healed" (James 5:16).

6. C.S. Lewis, *The Screwtape Letters* (New York, NY: Macmillan, 1944), p. 29.

7. Erwin Raphael McManus, *Uprising: A Revolution of the Soul* (Nashville, TN: Thomas Nelson, 2003), p. 11.

8. Galatians 5:13

Chapter 9—Walking Down Another Street

Epigraph. Dante Alighieri, quoted in Tim Alan Gardner, *The Naked Soul: God's Amazing, Everyday Solution to Loneliness* (Colorado Springs, CO: Waterbrook, 2004), p. 155.

1. For more on this, I highly recommend David Powlison, "Making All Things New: Restoring Pure Joy to the Sexually Broken," in John Piper and Justin Taylor, *Sex and the Supremacy of Christ* (Wheaton, IL: Crossway Books, 2005), pp. 65-106.

2. For one way this could look, see Nate Larkin, *Samson and the Pirate Monks: Calling Men to Authentic Brotherhood* (Nashville, TN: Thomas Nelson, 2006).

3. "If we confess our sins, he is faithful and just and will forgive us our sins and purify us from all unrighteousness" (1 John 1:9). This is in the present active tense, which implies a continuous action.

4. See 2 Corinthians 5:17 and Colossians 3:1-17 for examples of this.

5. For a practical guide to fighting sexual temptation, see Stephen Arterburn, Fred Stoeker, and Mike Yorkey, *Every Man's Battle: Every Man's Guide to Winning the War on Sexual Temptation One Victory at a Time* (Colorado Springs, CO: Waterbrook, 2000).

6. Psalm 51:1-5,7,10,12,15-17

7. "God's kindness leads you toward repentance" (Romans 2:4).

8. 2 Corinthians 10:3-5

9. Portia Nelson, *There's a Hole in My Sidewalk: The Romance of Self-Discovery* (Attria Books/Beyond Words, 1994).

10. Joshua Harris, *Not Even a Hint: Guarding Your Heart Against Lust* (Sisters, OR: Multnomah, 2003). p.42.

11. For a provocative look at the grace of God in relationship to sexual sin, take a look at Robert Farrar Capon's *Between Noon and Three: Romance, Law, and the Outrage of*

Grace (Grand Rapids, MI: Eerdmans, 1997). I don't agree with everything he suggests in his novel, but you can't help but come away from it reexamining our concept of grace.

12. John Piper, "How to Deal with the Guilt of Sexual Failure for the Glory of Christ and His Global Cause." Available online at www.desiringgod.org.

13. See Romans 5:1; 1 Corinthians 1:30; 6:11; 2 Corinthians 5:21

14. 2 Corinthians 5:17

15. Colossians 3:1-4

16. For example, Tim Alan Gardner's *The Naked Soul: God's Amazing, Everyday Solution to Loneliness* (Colorado Springs, CO: Waterbrook, 2004) is a great book on the subject of loneliness.

Chapter 10—Band of Brothers and Sisters

Epigraph. Larry Crabb with Don Hudson and Al Andrews, *The Silence of Adam: Becoming Men of Courage in a World of Chaos* (Grand Rapids, MI: Zondervan, 1995), p. 144.

1. This is paradox, not contradiction. We are not saying that God is one essence and three essences, or that God is one person and three persons. Those are contradictions. To say that God is one essence but three individuated persons is a mystery, but it is not contradictory.

2. Nancy Pearcey, *Total Truth: Liberating Christianity from Its Cultural Captivity* (Wheaton, IL: Crossway Books, 2004), pp. 132-34.

3. Arnold Fruchtenbaum, *Messianic Christology* (Tustin, CA: Ariel Ministries, 1998), pp. 102-16.

4. Matthew 3:16-17

5. See Philippians 2:6-11; Matthew 28:19-20.

6. For more on the implications of the Trinity for life and practice in the church, see Simon Chan, *Spiritual Theology: A Systematic Study of the Christian Life* (Downers Grove, IL: InterVarsity, 1998), pp. 45-50, 103-9. For a more technical discussion of the origins of the Trinity and a summary of current discussion, see also Alister E. McGrath, *Christian Theology*, 4th ed. (Oxford: Blackwell, 2007). Finally, see also Wayne Grudem, *Systematic Theology* (Grand Rapids, MI: Zondervan), 1994.

7. N.T. Wright, *Simply Christian: Why Christianity Makes Sense* (New York, NY: HarperSanFrancisco, 2006), p. 38.

8. The word *helper* is the word *ezer* in the Hebrew language. We can find it in Psalm 121:1-2: "I lift up my eyes to the hills—where does my help [*ezer*] come from? My help comes from the LORD, the Maker of heaven and earth." Psalm 89:19 says, "I have bestowed strength [*ezer*] on a warrior." In nearly every other instance in the Old Testament, when *helper* or *help* is used, it refers to God and the help that He supplies, particularly as a defense against adversaries. *Helper* is a strong word. Obviously, no

inferiority is implied. For further examples, see Deuteronomy 33:7,26,29; Psalm 20:2; 33:20; 70:5; 89:19-21 (NASB); 115:9-11; 124:8; 146:5; Hosea 13:9.

9. The words of Rolheiser on this point are fitting: "We are essentially social by nature. To be a human being is to be with others…Hell is not the other person, as Sartre once suggested, but the reverse. Our quest for God must be consistent with our nature. Hence, it must have, as a nonnegotiable part, a communitarian dimension. Ecclesiology, church, by definition, is precisely that, walking to God within a community. To attempt to make spirituality a private affair is to reject part of our very nature and walk inside of a loneliness that God himself has damned." Ronald Rolheiser, *The Holy Longing: The Search for a Christian Spirituality* (New York, NY: Doubleday, 1999), p. 135.

10. Rolheiser, *The Holy Longing,* pp. 128-29.

11. For more on this point, see Mike Erre, *The Jesus of Suburbia: Have We Tamed the Son of God to Fit Our Lifestyle?* (Nashville, TN: Thomas Nelson, 2006).

12. John 5:39-40

13. John Coe, of Talbot School of Theology's Institute for Spiritual Formation made this point in a Rock Harbor staff meeting.

14. John Eldredge, *The Way of the Wild Heart: A Map for the Masculine Journey* (Nashville TN: Thomas Nelson, 2006), p. 5.

15. Richard Rohr with Joseph Martos, *From Wild Man to Wise Man: Reflections on Male Spirituality* (Cincinnati, OH: Saint Anthony Messenger, 2005), p. 47.

16. Mark 3:31-35

17. Rohr speculates that God has us refer to Him as Father because the father wound is so prevalent.

18. Romans 8:15; Galatians 4:4-7

Chapter 11—Power and Control

Epigraph. Leon J. Podles, *The Church Impotent: The Feminization of Christianity* (Dallas, TX: Spence, 1999), p. xii.

1. Stu Weber, *Tender Warrior: God's Intention for a Man* (Sisters, OR: Multnomah, 1999), p. 92.

2. Larry Crabb, with Don Hudson and Al Andrews, *The Silence of Adam: Becoming Men of Courage in a World of Chaos* (Grand Rapids, MI: Zondervan, 1995), p. 117.

3. Ibid., pp. 124-25.

4. Crabb, *The Silence of Adam,* p. 55.

5. Pornography is an almost $60 billion a year industry in the U.S. today. For a look at the consequences of pornography on American society, I recommend Pamela Paul's book, *Pornified: How Pornography Is Transforming Our Lives, Our Relationships, and Our Families* (New York, NY: Times Books, 2005).

6. Rob Bell, *Sex God: Exploring the Endless Connections Between Sexuality and Spirituality* (Grand Rapids, MI: Zondervan, 2007), pp. 22-23.

7. For more on issues of power and control as they relate to the church, see Peter Scazzero's *The Emotionally Healthy Church: A Strategy for Discipleship that Actually Changes Lives* (Grand Rapids, MI: Zondervan, 2003), p. 117.

Chapter 12—The First and the Last

Epigraph. Thornton Wilder, *The Skin of Our Teeth: A Play* (New York, NY: Harper Perennial Modern Classics, 2003), quoted in Stephen Arterburn, *The Secrets Men Keep* (Nashville, TN: Integrity, 2006) p. 199.

1. The words used in the New Testament are *submit, be subject to, obey,* and *respect.* Peter says to submit for the Lord's sake to every human institution—government officials and believers at large (1 Peter 2:13-17), slave-owners and slaves (2:18-25), husbands and wives (3:1-7). All believers are called to submit to various authorities; it is part of their ultimate submission to Jesus Christ. Also, the universe is subject to Christ (Ephesians 1:22), Christ is subject to the Father (1 Corinthians 15:28), the church is subject to Christ (Ephesians 5:24), and Christians are subject to God (James 4:7). See Stu Weber, *Four Pillars of a Man's Heart: Bringing Strength into Balance* (Sisters, OR: Multnomah, 1997), pp. 75-76.

2. Sarah Sumner, *Men and Women in the Church* (Downers Grove, IL: InterVarsity, 2003), p. 157.

3. For more on these issues, see Ronald W. Pierce and Rebecca Merrill Groothuis, eds., *Discovering Biblical Equality: Complementarity Without Hierarchy* (Downers Grove, IL: IVP Academic, 2004), and John Piper and Wayne Grudem, eds., *Recovering Biblical Manhood and Womanhood: A Response to Evangelical Feminism* (Wheaton, IL: Crossway Books, 1991).

4. See, for example, Matthew 20:25-26.

5. For an excellent discussion of this point, see Leon J. Podles, *The Church Impotent: The Feminization of Christianity* (Dallas, TX: Spence, 1999), pp. 77-78.

6. For Jesus' treatment of women, see Aida Besancon Spencer, "Jesus' Treatment of Women in the Gospels," *Discovering Biblical Equality: Complementarity Without Hierarchy,* ed. Ronald W. Pierce and Rebecca Merrill Groothuis (Downers Grove, IL: IVP Academic, 2004), pp. 126-41.

7. Sumner, *Men and Women in the Church,* pp. 161-64.

8. Ephesians 5:32

9. John Eldredge, *The Way of the Wild Heart: A Map for the Masculine Journey* (Nashville, TN: Thomas Nelson, 2006), pp. 212-13.

10. John Eldredge, *Wild at Heart: Discovering the Secret of a Man's Soul* (Nashville, TN: Thomas Nelson, 2001), p. 177.

11. Stu Weber, *Tender Warrior* (Sisters, OR: Multnomah, 1993), p. 62.

12. See J.P. Moreland and Klaus Issler, *The Lost Virtue of Happiness: Discovering the Disciplines of the Good Life* (Colorado Springs, CO: Navpress, 2006).

13. Richard Rohr with Joseph Martos, *From Wild Man to Wise Man; Reflections on Male Spirituality* (Cincinnati, OH: Saint Anthony Messenger, 2005), p. 41.

14. This of course is true for women too, but how and why are different issues that lie beyond the scope of this discussion.

15. Nancy Pearcey, *Total Truth: Liberating Christianity from Its Cultural Captivity* (Wheaton, IL: Crossway Books, 2004), p. 328.

16. C.S. Lewis, *The Inspirational Writings of C.S. Lewis* (New York, NY: Inspirational Press, 1991), p. 400.

Chapter 13—Fatherhood, Biological or Otherwise

Epigraph. Ronald Rolheiser, "How Children Raise Their Parents," *Western Catholic Reporter*, March 27, 1995.

1. The real reason I hesitate is that both my wife (now) and my kids (someday) will read these words, and I don't want to eat them later.

2. When I use the terms *father, dad,* or *parent,* I mean to refer to anyone in a fathering relationship with someone else. Jesus taught that spiritual bonds are just as important (if not more so) than biological bonds (Mark 3:31-35), and Paul taught that the church functions as God's household and family (1 Timothy 3:15), so that we relate to each other as fathers, mothers, sons, and daughters (1 Timothy 5:1-2). That means that spiritual fathering is just as significant as biological fathering. The best case, of course, is that the two are combined, but that is increasingly becoming the exception rather than the rule.

3. This is to say nothing about the role of mothers in our society. Much could be written about that, but it obviously is beyond our intention here.

4. These statistics and their original sources can be found in various places. The ones I am using are borrowed from fathers.com/research.html, www.fatherhood.org/fatherfacts_t10.asp, and Stephen Arterburn, *The Secrets Men Keep* (Nashville, TN: Integrity, 2006), pp. 48-49.

5. See, for example, Proverbs 1:8.

6. I think the fact that I am a pastor makes my job harder, not easier. Many use the term *PK* to refer to how screwed up a lot of pastors' kids are.

7. Richard Rohr with Joseph Martos, *From Wild Man to Wise Man: Reflections on Male Spirituality* (Cincinnati, OH: Saint Anthony Messenger, 2005), p. 68.

8. Honoring, in most cases, also includes providing for them. Paul writes in 1 Timothy 5:8, "If anyone does not provide for his relatives, and especially for his immediate family, he has denied the faith and is worse than an unbeliever."

9. For some thought-provoking musings on the nature of the inner journey to wholeness, I recommend Parker J. Palmer, *A Hidden Wholeness: The Journey Toward an Undivided*

Life (San Francisco, CA: Jossey-Bass, 2004).

10. Teachers like J.P. Moreland, Rob Bell, and N.T. Wright have helped to bring this truth out for me. For more on this point, see Dallas Willard, *The Divine Conspiracy: Rediscovering Our Hidden Life in God* (New York, NY: HarperSanFrancisco, 1998).

11. I love what Rob Bell says about forgiveness: "Forgiveness is setting somebody free and then finding out that it was you." I don't know if the quote is original to him, but that's where I first heard it.

12. As my wife read that last sentence, she commented, "You were childish way before that." What would I do without her?

13. For those of us who need some help with raising boys to be solid Christian men, I recommend James Dobson, *Bringing Up Boys: Practical Advice and Encouragement for Those Shaping the Next Generation of Men*; John Eldredge, *The Way of the Wild Heart*; John Trent and Greg Johnson, *Dad's Everything Book for Sons*; Stephen Arterburn, Fred Stoeker, and Mike Yorkey, *Preparing Your Son for Every Man's Battle: Honest Conversations About Sexual Integrity*; and Dan Allender, *How Children Raise Parents: The Art of Listening to Your Family*.

14. Mark 12:28-30

15. Again, I feel somewhat stupid writing this because my kids are only ages four and two. Check back with me in ten years, and let's see how I'm doing.

16. I highly recommend Ella K. Lindvall's *Read Aloud Bible Stories* (Chicago, IL: Moody, 1995). She has written several volumes.

17. "Many overly strong men have weak sons because they squelch their kids. Sons must be disciplined to fulfill the cultural mandate in a masculine manner. The point of fathering is to channel and redirect their energy into an obedient response to the cultural mandate." Douglas Wilson, *Future Men* (Moscow, ID. Canon, 2001), p. 14.

18. Matthew 3:17

19. Matthew 17:1. Rohr comments, "Even Jesus needed to use the more daring, the more distant and the more dangerous word for God—"abba"—because that is where the wound is for so many." Rohr with Martos, *From Wild Man to Wise Man*, p. 69.

20. See Genesis 27.

21. John Eldredge, *The Way of the Wild Heart: A Map for the Masculine Journey* (Nashville TN: Thomas Nelson, 2006), p. 71.

22. Ibid., p. 5.

23. For more examples, see Robert Lewis, *Raising a Modern-Day Knight: A Father's Role in Guiding His Son to Authentic Manhood* (Wheaton, IL: Tyndale House, 1997).

24. Eldredge, *The Way of the Wild Heart*, p. 69.

25. I still have a hard time being fully present at home with my kids, entering into their world, playing what they want to play, and doing what they want to do. Often, quality time for us looks like going out to breakfast together or lying in bed together telling stories. In those moments I have a much easier time connecting with them.

Conclusion: Dissident Jesus

Epigraph. Andrew Greeley, "There's No Solving the Mystery of Christ," *Chicago Sun-Times,* January 24, 2004. Quoted in Mark Galli, *Jesus Mean and Wild: The Unexpected Love of an Untamable God* (Grand Rapids, MI: Baker Books, 2006), p. 19.

1. Many books are now beginning to capture this part of Jesus, including these: Mark Galli, *Jesus Mean and Wild: The Unexpected Love of an Untamable God* (Grand Rapids, MI: Baker Books, 2006); Mike Erre, *The Jesus of Suburbia; Have We Tamed the Son of God to Fit Our Lifestyle?* (Nashville, TN: Thomas Nelson, 2006); Paul Coughlin, *No More Christian Nice Guy: When Being Nice—Instead of Good—Hurts Men, Women, and Children* (Minneapolis, MN: Bethany House, 2005).

2. *Fox* was an insult, implying that Herod was conniving and weak.

3. For more on this, see Philip Yancey, *The Jesus I Never Knew* (Grand Rapids, MI: Zondervan, 1998).

4. See Coughlin, *No More Christian Nice Guy.*

5. Mark 2:17; 7:9; John 2:12-16; Matthew 10:21-39

6. An incredible book on this subject was recommended to me by Rob Bell. See Garret Keizer, *The Enigma of Anger: Essays on a Sometimes Deadly Sin* (San Francisco, CA: Jossey-Bass, 2002).

7. God often calls His people to this. See Deuteronomy 2:24-37 as an example.

8. Jesus wasn't a pacifist. See David Bivin, *New Light on the Difficult Words of Jesus: Insights from His Jewish Context* (Holland, MI: En-Gedi Resource Center, 2005), p. 103-8. Similarly, we misunderstand Jesus when He talks about turning the other cheek. To turn the other cheek does not mean to accept abuse; it means to not return evil for evil.

9. Ephesians 4:26

10. Keizer, *The Enigma of Anger,* p. 26.

11. Coughlin, *No More Christian Nice Guy,* p. 178. See also Proverbs 8:13: "To fear the LORD is to hate evil; I hate pride and arrogance, evil behavior and perverse speech."

12. Needless to say, we have so few examples of how this is done well in our world. Is proclaiming that Tinky Winky (of the TeleTubbies) is gay the way Jesus would have addressed the sexual confusion that reigns today? I don't think so. Nor would Jesus bomb abortion clinics or boycott Harry Potter. What would happen if Christians used the energy and money they spent on those things to free women sold into prostitution instead?

13. C.S. Lewis, *The Abolition of Man* (New York, NY: MacMillan, 1947).

A Brief Word to Pastors

Epigraph. Martin Luther, quoted in Joe Dallas, *The Gay Gospel? How Pro-Gay Advocates Misread the Bible* (Eugene, OR: Harvest House, 2007). The quote is right after the contents page.

1. Available online at www.churchformen.com/allmen.php. For a fuller explanation of the causes, effects, and possible solutions to this trend, see David Murrow, *Why Men Hate Going to Church* (Nashville, TN: Thomas Nelson, 2005). Other similar findings can be found at barna.org.

2. Leon J. Podles, *The Church Impotent: The Feminization of Christianity* (Dallas, TX: Spence, 1999), p. 3.

3. Interestingly, one study found that a significant characteristic of growing churches in the United States is that adult men comprise at least 60 percent of the congregation. You can find the study and results at www.uscongregations.org.

4. N.T. Wright, *Simply Christian: Why Christianity Makes Sense* (New York, NY: HarperSanFrancisco, 2006), pp. 236-37.

Bibliography

Allender, Dan B. *How Children Raise Parents: The Art of Listening to Your Family*. Colorado Springs, Co: Waterbrook, 1996.

Arterburn, Stephen. *The Secrets Men Keep*. Nashville, TN: Integrity, 2006.

Arterburn, Stephen, Fred Stoeker, and Mike Yorkey, *Every Man's Battle: Every Man's Guide to Winning the War on Sexual Temptation One Victory at a Time*. Colorado Springs, CO: Waterbrook, 2000.

Aterburn, Stephen, Fred Stoeker, and Mike Yorkey, *Preparing Your Son for Every Man's Battle: Honest Conversations About Sexual Integrity*. Colorado Springs, CO: Waterbrook, 2003.

Bell, Rob. *Sex God: Exploring the Endless Connections Between Sexuality and Spirituality* Grand Rapids, MI: Zondervan, 2007.

Bivin, David. *New Light on the Difficult Words of Jesus: Insights from His Jewish Context*. Holland, MI: En-Gedi Resource Center, 2005.

Bly, Robert. *Iron John*. Reading, MA: Addison-Wesley, 1990.

Brueggemann, Walter. *Peace*. St. Louis, MO: Chalice, 2001.

Capon, Robert Farrar. *Between Noon and Three: Romance, Law, and the Outrage of Grace*. Grand Rapids, MI: Eerdmans, 1997.

Chan, Simon. *Spiritual Theology: A Systematic Study of the Christian Life*. Downers Grove, IL: InterVarsity Press, 1998.

Coughlin, Paul. *No More Christian Nice Guy: When Being Nice—Instead of Good—Hurts Men, Women, and Children*. Minneapolis, MN: Bethany, 2005.

Crabb, Larry. *Men and Women: Enjoying the Difference*. Grand Rapids, MI: Zondervan, 1991.

Crabb, Larry, with Don Hudson and Al Andrews. *The Silence of Adam: Becoming Men of Courage in a World of Chaos*. Grand Rapids, MI: Zondervan, 1995.

Dallas, Joe. *The Gay Gospel? How Pro-Gay Advocates Misread the Bible*. Eugene, OR: Harvest House, 2007.

Dobson, James. *Bringing Up Boys: Practical Advice and Encouragement for Those Shaping the Next Generation of Men*. Wheaton, IL: Tyndale House, 2001.

Eldredge, John. *The Way of the Wild Heart: A Map for the Masculine Journey*. Nashville TN: Nelson Books, 2006.

Eldredge, John. *Wild at Heart: Discovering the Secret of a Man's Soul*. Nashville: TN, Thomas Nelson, 2001.

Erre, Mike. *The Jesus of Suburbia; Have We Tamed the Son of God to Fit Our Lifestyle?*. Nashville, TN: Thomas Nelson, 2006.

Exley, Richard. *Man of Valor: Every Man's Quest for a Life of Honor, Conviction, and Character.* Lakeland, FL: White Stone Books, 2005.

Fee, Gordon D. *Paul, the Spirit, and the People of God.* Peabody, MA: Hendrickson, 1996.

Galli, Mark. *Jesus Mean and Wild: The Unexpected Love of an Untamable God.* Grand Rapids, MI: Baker Books, 2006.

Gardner, Tim Alan. *The Naked Soul: God's Amazing, Everyday Solution to Loneliness.* Colorado Springs, CO: Waterbrook, 2004.

Hegeman, David Bruce. *Plowing in Hope: Toward a Biblical Theology of Culture.* Moscow, ID: Canon, 1999.

Hood, Xan. *Untamed: Becoming the Man You Want to Be.* Colorado Springs, CO: TH1NK, 2006.

Keizer, Garret. *The Enigma of Anger: Essays on a Sometimes Deadly Sin.* San Francisco, CA: Jossey-Bass, 2002.

Kidner, Derek. *Genesis: An Introduction and Commentary.* Downers Grove, IL: InterVarsity, 1967.

Kreeft, Peter. *How to Win the Culture War: A Christian Battle Plan for a Society in Crisis.* Downers Grove, IL: InterVarsity, 2002.

Larkin, Nate. *Samson and the Pirate Monks: Calling Men to Authentic Brotherhood.* Nashville, TN: Thomas Nelson, 2006.

Lewis, C.S. *The Abolition of Man.* New York, NY: MacMillan, 1947.

Lewis, C.S. *The Inspirational Writings of C.S. Lewis.* New York, NY: Inspirational Press, 1991.

Lewis, C.S. *The Screwtape Letters.* New York, NY: Macmillan, 1944.

Lewis, Robert. *Raising a Modern-Day Knight: A Father's Role in Guiding His Son to Authentic Manhood.* Wheaton, IL: Tyndale House, 1997.

Lewis, Robert, and William Hendricks. *Rocking the Roles: Building a Win-Win Marriage.* Colorado Springs, CO: NavPress, 1991.

Longman III, Tremper. *How to Read Genesis.* Downers Grove, IL: InterVarsity, 2005.

McGrath, Alister E. *Christian Theology,* 4th ed.. Oxford: Blackwell, 2007.

McManus, Erwin Raphael. *Uprising: A Revolution of the Soul.* Nashville, TN: Thomas Nelson, 2003.

Moreland, J. P., and Klaus Issler. *The Lost Virtue of Happiness: Discovering the Disciplines of the Good Life.* Colorado Springs, CO: Navpress, 2006.

Mouw, Richard J. *He Shines on All That's Fair: Culture and Common Grace.* Grand Rapids, MI: Eerdmans, 2001.

Murrow, David. *Why Men Hate Going to Church*. Nashville, TN: Nelson Books, 2005.

Nelson, Tommy, *Book of Romance: What Solomon Says About Love, Sex, and Intimacy*. New York, NY: Thomas Nelson, 1998.

Palmer, Parker J. *A Hidden Wholeness: The Journey Toward an Undivided Life*. San Francisco, CA: Jossey-Bass, 2004.

Palmer, Parker J. *Let Your Life Speak: Listening to the Voice of Vocation*. San Francisco, CA: Jossey-Bass, 2000.

Paul, Pamela. *Pornified: How Pornography Is Transforming Our Lives, Our Relationships, and Our Families*. New York, NY: Times Books, 2005.

Pearcey, Nancy. *Total Truth: Liberating Christianity from Its Cultural Captivity*. Wheaton, IL: Crossway Books, 2004.

Pierce, Ronald W., and Rebecca Merrill Groothuis, eds. *Discovering Biblical Equality: Complementarity Without Hierarchy*. Downers Grove, IL: IVP Academic, 2004.

Piper, John. *What's the Difference?: Manhood and Womanhood Defined According to the Bible*. Wheaton, IL: Crossway Books, 1990.

Piper, John, and Justin Taylor. *Sex and the Supremacy of Christ*. Wheaton, IL: Crossway Books, 2005.

Piper, John, and Wayne Grudem, eds. *Recovering Biblical Manhood and Womanhood: A Response to Evangelical Feminism*. Wheaton, IL: Crossway Books, 1991.

Plantinga Jr., Cornelius. *Engaging God's World: A Christian Vision of Faith, Learning, and Living*. Grand Rapids, MI: Eerdmans, 2002.

Plantinga Jr., Cornelius. *Not the Way It's Supposed to Be: A Breviary of Sin*. Grand Rapids, MI: Eerdmans, 1995.

Podles, Leon J. *The Church Impotent: The Feminization of Christianity*. Dallas, TX: Spence, 1999.

Riter, Tim. *Strong Enough to Be a Man: Reclaiming God's Plan for Masculinity*. Kansas City, MO: Beacon Hill, 2005.

Rolheiser, Ronald. *The Holy Longing: The Search for a Christian Spirituality*. New York, NY: Doubleday, 1999.

Rohr, Richard, with Joseph Martos. *From Wild Man to Wise Man; Reflections on Male Spirituality*. Cincinnati, OH: Saint Anthony Messenger, 2005.

Sarna, Nahum M. *Understanding Genesis: The World of the Bible in the Light of History*. New York, NY: Schocken Books, 1966.

Scazzero, Peter. *Emotionally Healthy Spirituality: Unleash a Revolution in Your Life in Christ*. Nashville, TN: Integrity, 2007.

Scazzero, Peter, with Warren Bird. *The Emotionally Healthy Church: A Strategy for Discipleship That Actually Changes Lives*. Grand Rapids, MI: Zondervan, 2003.

Seay, Chris, and Chad Karger. *To Become One*. Lake Mary, FL: Relevant Books, 2004.

Smith, Stephen W., ed. *The Transformation of a Man's Heart.* Downer's Grove, IL: InterVarsity, 2006.

Stephens, Steve. *The Wounded Warrior: A Survival Guide for When You're Beat Up, Burned Out, or Battle Weary.* Sisters, OR: Multnomah, 2006.

Sumner, Sarah. *Men and Women in the Church.* Downers Grove, IL: InterVarsity, 2003.

Trent, John, and Greg Johnson, *Dad's Everything Book for Sons: Practical Ideas for a Quality Relationship.* Grand Rapids, MI: Zondervan, 2003.

Walton, John H. *Genesis: NIV Application Commentary.* Grand Rapids, MI: Zondervan, 2001.

Weber, Stu. *Four Pillars of a Man's Heart: Bringing Strength into Balance.* Sisters, OR: Multnomah, 1997.

Weber, Stu. *Tender Warrior: God's Intention for a Man.* Sisters, OR: Multnomah, 1999.

Wilson, Douglas. *Future Men.* Moscow, ID: Canon, 2001.

Winner, Lauren. *Real Sex: The Naked Truth About Chastity.* Grand Rapids, MI: Brazos, 2005.

Wittmer, Michael E. *Heaven Is a Place on Earth: Why Everything You Do Matters to God.* Grand Rapids, MI: Zondervan, 2004.

Wright, N.T. *Simply Christian: Why Christianity Makes Sense.* New York, NY: HarperSanFrancisco, 2006.

Yancey, Philip. *The Jesus I Never Knew.* Grand Rapids, MI: Zondervan, 1995.

World...

And People Are Talking About It...